Stewardship economy   4

the economy, wealth and

universal income

Julian Pratt

Published by

Editorial note

This book brings together previously unpublished material which Julian worked on alongside the summary book, *Stewardship Economy 1: private property without private ownership*. With the other five books in the series, it provides the additional material that lies behind the proposals and assertions made in book 1. Unfortunately, aspects of this work are unfinished, some of the examples provided are out of date, there is some repetition of text and some references (bibliography in book 7) are not available. I hope you, the reader, will excuse this and will find the work as a whole thought-provoking and topical.

Rosemary Field

September 2021

ISBN 978-14717-0179-5

Contents

Stewardship Economy

The Stewardship Economy series of books questions one of the foundations on which market-based economies rest: the system of property rights. It suggests that the form of private property that works well for the things that we make is both unethical and inefficient when we apply it to land and the rest of the natural world. It proposes an alternative to ownership – stewardship.

The underlying principle of stewardship is that everyone is entitled to an equal share of the wealth of the natural world. The steward of any part of the natural world has the secure and exclusive right to use it, the responsibility to care for it and the duty to compensate others for excluding them from it.

In practical terms this means that stewards of land pay fees that are equal to its market rent. These fees provide revenue that may be used to provide government with an income that is an alternative to orthodox taxation and, ideally, to provide everyone with a (small) Universal Income. Stewards of environmental resources pay fees equal to their resource rent, and this revenue is distributed to everyone as an Environmental Dividend.

Books in the series

Stewardship Economy 1: private property without private ownership is the first book and provides an overall summary of the main ideas.

Stewardship Economy 2: Valuing land and managing transition sets out in some detail how to establish the market rent of land and how to make the transition from an ownership to a stewardship economy. It also considers how the revenue from stewardship fees might be distributed.

the revenue from stewardship fees might be distributed.

Stewardship Economy 3: Land, environment and climate explores how a stewardship economy would transform the way we use land, provide housing and develop our cities. It goes on to consider how stewardship would help address pressing environmental and climate concerns.

Stewardship Economy 4: The economy, wealth and universal income (this book) focuses on the impact of stewardship on the national and global economy, how the distribution of wealth would be changed and the impact of a Universal Income.

Stewardship Economy 5: efficient, fair taxes and the role of the state describes the some of the adverse effects of our current system of taxation and considers the role of the state in a stewardship economy.

Stewardship Economy 6: property rights describes the systems of property rights in our current economic system, their history and how property rights could be more fair and efficient in a stewardship economy.

Stewardship Economy 7: some economics explained, economic terms and bibliography. This book provides an introduction to some key economic concepts for the non-specialist and lists the references, as far as they are available.

Introduction

This book in the Stewardship Economy series focuses on the impact of stewardship on the national and global economy, how the distribution of wealth would be changed and the impact of a Universal Income.

Part I considers stewardship and the national economy. Chapter 1 discusses the business environment for firms and for charities. Chapter 2 explores the question of how the money supply and banking might be managed in a stewardship economy. Chapters 3 to 5 look at different aspects of the efficiency of the economy. Chapter 3 takes a short-term static equilibrium view and describes how stewardship makes both the land market and taxation more efficient. Chapter 4 takes a long-term view and looks at how stewardship would affect the capacity of the economy to sustain long-term growth, if that is what is wanted. And Chapter 5 describes how stewardship would provide medium-term macroeconomic stability.

Part II considers the global economy. Chapter 6 discusses international issues such as free trade and protectionism, exchange rates, population movements and transfers to Low Consumption Economies. It then explores the possibilities provided in the situation where stewardship has been adopted by more than one state and where stewardship fees are shared across national boundaries. Chapter 7 explores issues of particular importance to Low Consumption Economies such as poverty and land rights.

In Part III focuses on how income and wealth is distributed in a stewardship economy and compares this with the distribution in an ownership economy.

Part IV describes options for the use of revenue from stewardship fees and sets out some illustrative examples. Chapters 10 and 11 consider how a Universal Income might work, and the benefits. Chapter 12 then looks briefly at how investing in infrastructure could benefit all.

The full bibliography is in book 7.

Part I   UK Economy

Chapter 1 Business and charities

Which sorts of business will be more profitable in a stewardship economy, and which less profitable? What system of regulation and red tape will be required? How will charities fare when they have no tax advantages over other businesses?

Ownership economy

Business

All firms pay for the land they use, whether as payments of rent to a landlord, mortgage interest to a bank or as the opportunity cost of the investment that they have made in the land.

In ownership economies business bears a significant burden of taxation. The National Non-Domestic (Business) Rate is a cost to the business, Corporation Tax reduces net profits directly and National Insurance Contributions increase the cost of employing people and act as a tax on jobs. Income Tax and VAT are not taxes on business, but Income Tax reduces the value of dividends and wages, and VAT reduces demand for the firm's products by increasing the price paid by the customer. Both of these have a negative impact on business.

For a worker to achieve a certain level of take-home pay, their employer will be paying two or three times this amount when Income Tax, National Insurance, sick pay and so on are taken into account.

As well as the financial cost, taxation distorts business decision-making and accounting. It causes firms to place undue emphasis on minimising tax bills rather than on maximising profits.

Conventional taxes bring a cost in time and aggravation as well as money, as anyone who has collected and remitted National Insurance Contributions, PAYE and VAT knows only too well. VAT imposes an administrative burden, inspections, penalties and accountability mechanisms that are an irritant to most businesses. The burden of administering PAYE and National Insurance Contributions falls largely on employers.

Businesses have to prepare accounts that serve the purposes of the tax system, for example incorporating arbitrary rates for writing off the cost of capital goods, not their own need to understand the financial state of the company. Any reward for an employee, like a Christmas bonus or company car, has to be accounted for tax purposes.

Red tape extends beyond the direct impact of administering the tax system and the accounts required for tax purposes to the employment protection measures that have to be adopted.

In an ownership economy, security of income is provided by security of employment (or self-employment). So, it's not surprising that, in ownership economies, we require employers to provide income when an employee is sick or on maternity or paternity leave; to follow strict procedures before dismissing an employee either because they are unsuited to the job or on the grounds of redundancy; and to provide compensation payments for redundancy.

These requirements make the labour market remarkably inflexible. Employers may be reluctant to take on new permanent staff unless they are confident of being able to provide long-term employment.

Ownership economies are not particularly conducive to part-time working, not least because most people need full-time pay to make ends meet. In addition, the National Insurance system and employment protection measures encourage employers to expand working hours by offering overtime to existing workers rather than part-time work to new recruits.

Firms are required to contribute to their employees' pensions, and this imposes a further economic burden. Inadequate payments into pension funds and (in the U.S) health care plans, particularly 'holidays' taken in times of rising stock markets, have bankrupted many companies.

Rates of pay

Classical economic theory supposed that, at times when people were generally spending little – times of low aggregate demand –

wages would fall and, given a perfect market with equilibrium conditions, workers would price themselves back into work. When wages are so low that many workers need top-up Tax Credits, it is not surprising that they fail to behave in this way and protest against falling rates of pay and the associated unfairness.

In ownership economies the most enjoyable jobs tend to the best paid. A survey for the Industrial Society in 2000 (Operational Research Newsletter 2001:5) reported that 70 per cent of those earning over £70,000 a year would carry on working even if they had enough money to live as comfortably as they liked, while only 52 per cent of all workers would keep their jobs if they came into money. This suggests that ownership economies overpay those who have the best-paid jobs – perhaps their pay is not determined simply by 'market forces' but by other factors.

Cost of land

The government's national accounts (the Blue Book) distinguishes between rent (payments made for the use of land and the natural world) and rental (payments made for the use of fixed assets like buildings, machines and vehicles) (Office for National Statistics 1998: 628).

In an ownership economy the tenant of a property makes a payment, commonly called the 'rent', which is a combination of rent for the land and rental for the buildings. Rent for the land is usually close to its market rent, though it may lag behind in times of rising land values and this may be exacerbated by legislation fixing 'fair rents' at below market values. The rent paid for land may exceed the market rent in times of falling land values, and this may be exacerbated by rent clauses that protect the landlord by requiring all rent revisions to be upwards.

The 'rent' that a landlord receives comprises rent for the land and rental for the buildings. An owner-occupier pays interest on the mortgage that they took out to buy the property. At the time of purchase this interest is broadly equal to the market rent. As the market rent rises over the years an owner-occupier pays progressively less for the use of the land than does a tenant. Very often owner-occupiers make less efficient use of land than landlords or tenants, who experience land costs directly in their accounts.

Environmental charges

In an ownership economy environmental charges are widely considered to be bureaucratic and anti-business. This is true for sectors of the economy that are profitable in the short-term only because their costs are externalised and they are causing long-term damage to the environment and so, ultimately, to the economy. For any firm that takes account of their environmental impact, environmental charges that are faced by the whole sector provide them with a competitive advantage.

Charities and faith groups

Charities in ownership economies are exempt from a range of taxes including Income Tax on bank interest, royalties, land, property and a range of trading activities. Charities are eligible for a reduction in the National Non-Domestic (Business) Rate of at least 80 per cent, and eligible for relief from VAT on some products. Most importantly, donations to charities are exempt from Income Tax, so the government subsidises each donation from a taxpayer by 20-50 per cent. Exemptions and reductions amount to a subsidy of over £1 billion each year from the government, and so from the taxpayer.

There is widespread support for the idea that taxpayers should fund charitable aims that are selected by individuals who are giving their own money to benefit others. But there are also concerns where large charitable donors are determining a significant amount of government expenditure.

The controversies go well beyond the support provided to private fee-paying schools. The second-largest charity in the world is the Dutch-registered Stichting Ingka Foundation whose purpose is to support 'innovation in the field of architectural and interior design'. It is not legally required to publish any accounts but investigations by the Economist (13/5/06:75) reported that the foundation, which owns the parent company of IKEA, devotes itself largely to building its own reserves (with the help of the government subsidies) in case IKEA needs investment capital.

Stewardship economy

Business

A stewardship economy is vastly more business-friendly than an ownership economy. There are no taxes and greatly reduced red tape. Wages may be lower, at least for the highest earners, and labour is more flexible. The cost of land is more-or-less unchanged for most businesses other than those who were landowners in an ownership economy.

Apart from stewardship fees, and charges for environmental permits, firms would pay no taxes at all in an established stewardship economy. This makes the firm more profitable.

In the absence of Income Tax and National Insurance Contributions firms have the opportunity to cut gross rates of pay while leaving take-home pay unchanged or increased (see below). The absence of VAT means either that the firm's products are cheaper for customers or that there is a greater profit margin. The firm earns greater net profits as there is no Corporation Tax. Its dividends are more valuable because there is no Income Tax payable, and any rise in the share price is undiluted by Capital Gains Tax.

As firms are more profitable, they can employ and supply more people and they contribute to greater economic output than in an ownership economy. The most dramatic impact is at the geographical sites where production is least favourable, the margin of production, as a business can flourish here that would simply be impossible to conduct in the tax environment of an ownership economy.

The **change in profitability** of a firm, if it found itself transported from an ownership economy to a stewardship economy, would depend on whether it had been a tenant, landlord or owner-occupier.

A firm that had leased its property (buildings and land) from a landlord in an ownership economy might continue the arrangement. The landlord becomes a steward, the firm remains a tenant paying rent and rental, and its costs are unchanged. Or the landlord might sell the buildings to the firm, which would take over the stewardship of the property. In this case it would pay the market rent of the land not to a landlord but to the Land Stewardship Trust as stewardship fees. Its land costs are unchanged. If it took out a mortgage to pay for the buildings, the interest will not be dissimilar from the cost of leasing the buildings. (If it paid for the buildings from its own reserves the situation would be very similar as it would be forgoing the interest that it otherwise would have been earning on these reserves). With its costs largely unchanged and completely free from existing taxes, the firm would be far more profitable than in an ownership economy.

Things are very different for a firm that currently makes its profits by acting as a landlord and leasing out property. Transported to a stewardship economy it would still own its buildings and be able to derive a rental income from leasing them out tax-free. But its land would be worthless, as it would have to pay stewardship fees that are equal to the market rent of its land. The absence of Inheritance Tax, Capital Gains Tax, National Insurance and VAT would only partially compensate for this loss. A rapid transition to a stewardship economy would amount to confiscation of the land value, which would be unacceptable.

Many firms in ownership economies both own and use their properties and, if rapidly transported, the firm would face stewardship fees that are a new cost to the firm and would wipe out the market value of any land that they own. The firm would, however, benefit from the removal of the wide range of taxes that bear on it.

All firms that use land in a stewardship economy make regular payments equal to its market rent, whether this is to a landlord as rent or to the Land Stewardship Trust as stewardship fees. This is an intended outcome of stewardship. It makes land unattractive as an investment unless it is being used productively enough to generate the market rent and so to pay the stewardship fees. This releases under-used land on to the market, so in a stewardship economy there is more land available to entrepreneurs.

In the imaginary case of an instantaneous transition to a stewardship economy some businesses would be more profitable than they are in an ownership economy (those that are currently tenants, and owner-occupiers that own small amounts of low-value land) while others would be less profitable (those who are currently landlords, and owner-occupiers that own large amounts of high value land).

In practice transition from ownership to stewardship would involve the replacement of existing business property taxes (National Non-Domestic (Business) Rates) by stewardship fees.

There are several aspects of a stewardship economy that influence wage levels including its impact on economic activity, freedom from taxes on jobs and the receipt of a Universal Income.

Employers find that the economy is more buoyant and a greater proportion of those who want to work are doing so. They have to do more to compete for good workers, which tends to push wages up. The absence of Income Tax and National Insurance Contributions may lead to lower labour costs, or to higher take-home pay, or both.

Workers receive a small private income as a Universal Income, so wages are never a worker's only source of income. This makes it worth people's while to take up low-paid and part-time work and the unemployment and benefit traps disappear.

This is a blessing for employers, but something of a mixed blessing. Workers may be prepared to work for lower wages as they already have a small private income – but equally they may be less inclined to work, or may demand higher pay, as they are not as dependent on employment as they are in an ownership economy. It may be more important in a stewardship economy to provide work that people find intrinsically satisfying to do.

A stewardship economy makes it easier for people to work part-time, and that may become the dominant pattern of employment. It should be easier for workers to leave a job that they do not like or to which they are not well suited. Workers are likely to be more flexible about taking up and leaving employment and there is little or no need for a whole raft of employment protection measures.

In an established stewardship economy unemployment is difficult to define or measure, as nob receives unemployment benefits. Employers find that there are fewer barriers to creating jobs, so work is easier to find.

Given a Universal Income, some people might not want to seek work at all, while others might want to work part-time at times when this suits their needs for work-life balance. 'Employment' has much more porous boundaries.

A person's security is derived, at least in part, from their Universal Income, not from security of employment, so employment protection measures including redundancy payments may not be necessary. The ability to dismiss staff who are no longer needed would encourage employers to take on more staff when business opportunities present themselves.

The **lack of taxes** reduces the amount of time and effort businesses put into running the tax and benefits system – particularly VAT, National Insurance Contributions and PAYE. Businesses of course need to prepare accounts in a stewardship economy, but there is no need to prepare tax accounts – no need to use arbitrary rates of writing off the cost of capital goods, no need to separate out expenses like entertaining that are not tax-allowable. The effort of accounting is significantly reduced, allowing the accounts to focus more on understanding the business.

Of course, businesses will need to give some time to attend to the workings of stewardship. They will need to inform the Land Stewardship Trust when they make improvements or add new buildings and will need to scrutinise the annual revaluations of their stewardship fees and decide whether to appeal. But in all sorts of ways the lack of taxes in a stewardship economy reduces the amount of red tape experienced by businesses.

In the realm of **environmental protection,** too, there should be some reduction in red tape as market mechanisms and true cost pricing take on some of the work that regulation plays in ownership economies. Environmental charges are intended to change behaviour, of firms as well as of individuals. True cost pricing of inputs like fossil fuels and water will have two sorts of impact on firms.

The first is that it provides an incentive to all firms to do all they can to use these inputs with the greatest possible technical efficiency. The other is that, where the use of the inputs is unavoidable, competing firms face the same costs as long as they use their inputs with equal technical efficiency. This means that they can, and do, pass the cost on to the consumer who will then feel a financial pressure to reduce their level of consumption. Environmental charges do not reduce any individual firm's competitive advantage, but all affected firms face declining sales.

Rates of pay are likely to be quite different from those in ownership economies, but both the general level of pay and pay differentials are difficult to predict.

Demand from employers for labour will probably be higher in a stewardship economy than in an ownership economy as the economy would be more buoyant due to the absence of the deadweight loss of taxation, especially in areas that are at the margin of production. On the one hand, the supply of labour may be lower as some workers reduce the hours they work because they are receiving a Universal Income and as more people have some land of their own and can earn at least some income from it. On the other hand, the supply of labour may be higher as people find it easier to take on part-time work.

People might accept, when necessary, lower pay if their basic living expenses are met by a Universal Income. The Universal Income may also remove or reduce the need for minimum wage legislation.

This combination of factors means that the general level of pay in a stewardship economy might be higher or lower than in an ownership economy. It would depend on whether people like their jobs, and how they handle the trade-off between leisure time and the purchase of non-essentials.

It would be possible to estimate people's propensity to work in the new situation, once information is available about the probable levels of stewardship fees and Universal Income, using methods such as questionnaires, choice experiments and simulations.

In a stewardship economy people in high-paid jobs would probably want to continue to do enjoyable work, while people in low-paid jobs might need to be offered higher levels of pay to provide an incentive to work. So, wage differentials might be narrower.

Charities and faith groups

In a stewardship economy charities and faith groups that own their own properties or lease them at below market rent face a cost that they do not have in an ownership economy; they need to pay stewardship fees for their properties. The state must not exempt them from stewardship fees as this would favour those charities that currently own rather than lease their properties and would provide an incentive to transfer land into charitable hands, distorting the allocation and use of land as well as leading to unpredictable losses of revenue.

In a stewardship economy the state provides no subsidy to charities through exemptions from stewardship fees and they lose their tax advantage as there are no taxes to be exempt from. This loss of financial advantage to charities might be – to some extent - compensated for by increased donations from individuals with greater disposable income once they are free from Income Tax.

A libertarian version of stewardship might accept this situation, but socialist and liberal versions would want the state to support charities either on the grounds that these benefit society as a whole or that they provide people with their rights – to freedom, education, access to the environment or whatever.

This assumes that, whether in an ownership economy or a stewardship economy, the current levels of government support are approximately correct, amounting to £3.4 billion per year through tax breaks to donors and charities themselves (Economist: 9/6/12). The wisdom and level of this support is currently disputed. Subsidies allow wealthy donors to leverage government support for their personal choice of interventions in the world, some of which (for example private schools) benefit primarily the rich themselves.

As an alternative to tax breaks the state could provide a subsidy directly to the charity, and the role of the Charity Commissioners would then be to assess the eligibility of each charity for this subsidy. There are many possible alternative ways of providing such a subsidy – for example in proportion to some measure of their impact, the number of hours worked by unpaid volunteers, the total receipts from small donors or another chosen measure of their worthiness for state support.

This would be much fairer than the present system, in which the state subsidises the donations of wealthy (top-rate) taxpayers by more than twice as much as low-rate taxpayers, while non-taxpayers and street collections get no subsidy at all. It would also be more transparent, and it would reduce the paperwork that charities need to provide claim Gift Aid by documenting that the donors are identifiable UK taxpayers.

Where charities are in direct competition with the private sector they would retain the advantage that they have as the direct result of gifts of time and money, and of any state subsidy. But they would lose the commercial advantage over the private sector that is provided in an ownership economy by the tax breaks that they enjoy.

Charities that might face particular challenges in a stewardship economy are those that are responsible for the stewardship of significant landholdings such as the National Trust, Royal Society for the Protection of Birds and the Woodland Trust. These charities would face stewardship fees on their land. The key to keeping the stewardship fees of charities and faith groups down to manageable levels is the planning system. If a church is required by planning regulations to be used as a place of worship, or at least is prevented from being used for commercial or domestic use, its stewardship fees will be much lower than if it was free from these planning provisions. If there are strict restrictions on development, and requirements about the quality of estate management, charities like the National Trust are unlikely to have serious competitors vying for their land and bidding up the stewardship fees. These stewardship fees might be low or indeed negative, taking the form of a subsidy where the requirements for access and environmental management are onerous.

Chapter 2 Money and banking

There are two reasons for discussing money and banking in a book about property rights in the natural world. The first is that the price of land is directly related to the supply of credit. To take an extreme example, if there were no institutions engaged in mortgage lending then prospective house buyers could offer no more than their current savings to buy a home, and the price of the land on which houses are built would be much lower than it now is. Since bank lending is usually secured on the collateral value of property, if land values were lower banks would be able to lend less.

The other connection between land and money is that the private property right to land is a monopoly (exclusive) right granted by government. Once questions have been raised about land ownership, there are inevitably questions about the way in which the government allocates other monopoly rights including the right to create money.

This chapter identifies the problems caused by the current way in which the money supply is created and controlled by retail and commercial banks, known as fractional reserve banking. It explores the benefits we might expect if this were to be replaced in a stewardship economy by full reserve banking in which the state takes direct responsibility for creating the money supply.

Money

Ownership economy

Money is a medium of exchange, that is to say, a mechanism for making a payment or repaying a debt. It makes it possible to trade without all the inconvenience of barter. Other functions of money, as a measure of value (unit of account) and as a store of value, only arise from its role in exchange.

Origins of money

Most legal tender is issued by the state, which levies taxes and determines the currency in which they will be paid. Charles Goodhart has suggested that the state issues money not merely to facilitate trade and production but to make economic activity susceptible to taxation (Charles Goodhart 1998).

Coins have been issued by the state since 650 BCE http://rg.ancients.info/lion/article.html and paper money was issued by the state in China in 860 AD https://www.pbs.org/wgbh/nova/article/history-money/.

In Europe, however, paper money originated independently of the state as promissory notes issued by goldsmiths (and subsequently banks) to their depositors. These became a medium of exchange and were printed in such quantities that in the UK the Bank Charter Act (1844) was enacted to reduce inflation by granting to the Bank of England the sole right to issue banknotes in England. This ensured that the entire money supply was created by the state, in the form of notes and coin.

In recent years new currencies have arisen that are not legal tender including, most significantly, cryptocurrencies such as Bitcoin that are based on blockchain technology.

In ownership economies the state delegates the monopoly right to create money to retail and commercial banks – it grants a franchise to create money using the mechanism called fractional reserve banking.

Fractional reserve banking

Since the 19th century money has increasingly taken the form not of paper or coin but of the accounts that depositors hold with retail and commercial banks. By 1946, when the Bank of England was nationalised, 50 per cent of the money in circulation took the form of notes and coin (legal tender). As of 31 October 2010, the monthly average of outstanding notes and coins was £57.7 billion while the monthly average of amounts outstanding of banks' deposits with the Bank of England was £143 billion, i.e., notes and coins amounted to 29 per cent of the total.

https://www.whatdotheyknow.com/request/percentage_of_real_money_vs_digi.

The money in the digital records of banks is not created by the state, but by banks themselves. The creation occurs at the instant when a bank makes a loan, as interest-bearing debt, to an individual or business. This is called the fractional reserve system of banking because the banks cannot create money at will but have to retain, in the form of cash or deposits with the central (reserve) bank, a specified fraction of the amount of money that they hold on deposit. This mechanism, under which the state grants a franchise to the banks that allows them to create money, is at once so simple that it is described in basic economic textbooks (e.g., Paul Samuelson & William Nordhaus (1992: 508) and so astonishing that it is difficult to believe that any such mechanism could have arisen. Indeed, only 15 percent of UK members of parliament are aware what is going on www.positivemoney.org/2017/10/mp-poll. There are videos available that make the mechanism very understandable www.positivemoney.org/videos.

Disadvantages of fractional reserve banking

There are several major disadvantages of fractional reserve banking when compared with a system in which the money supply is created directly by the state. It deprives the central bank of direct control over the money supply, distorts interest rates, fuels the cycles of boom and bust in the property market, diverts investment into property and away from enterprise, subsidises the banks at the expense of the taxpayer, increases the risk of bank failure and requires people to take on debt in order to provide a medium of exchange:

The Bank of England has two ways of controlling the money supply directly. It can issue physical currency as notes and coins. Or it can issue money electronically by writing it in to its own account or that of one of its depositors, such as the government – as it has done from time to time since 2009 in its programme of quantitative easing. The Bank of England can also influence the money supply indirectly, though this introduces delays and uncertainties. One intervention that changes the money supply is to alter the reserve ratio, though this is a longer-term measure usually carried out to stabilise the retail banks.

But the Bank of England's chosen way to influence the money supply is by manipulating interest rates and so the level of demand for bank-created credit. Lowering the interest rate increases the level of demand for money and the banks create more of it. This also reduces people's propensity to save. Raising the interest rate reduces the level of demand for money and people curb their appetite for credit just as savings are stimulated.

Distorts interest rates

This manipulation of interest rates, whether by setting the base rate or by buying and selling government bonds (open market operations), gives the Bank of England only a very imperfect way of influencing how much credit the banks create. For entirely practical, as well as political, reasons the Bank of England is not in a position effectively to damp down asset prices, particularly land values, when necessary by raising interest rates. These interest rates would have to be higher than the rate of growth in asset values, and during a boom such high interest rates would damage business both by increasing the cost of finance and by raising the exchange rate.

On the other hand, when the economy is shrinking and the Bank would like to provide a monetary stimulus, lowering interest rates is also often ineffective as it fails to lead to an expansion of bank credit – either because banks are unwilling to lend, or customers are unwilling to borrow. This was the experience of Japan in the 1990s, when the banks were nursing losses from the collapse of a property bubble and were rebuilding their assets. Once nominal interest rates have fallen to zero it is challenging to lower them any further.

This manipulation of interest rates, as well as being ineffective, introduces market inefficiencies by distorting the market's perception of risk and of the importance of the future. If the government pays interest on risk-free investments, investors come to assume that it is possible to earn interest without taking a risk.

If control of the money supply requires an increase in interest rates this will also increase the rate at which investors, particularly the state, discount the future when making cost-benefit calculations. As a result, the consequences of long-term environmental damage are not taken into account.

Interest rate distortion also distorts exchange rates, leading to an overvalued currency when interest rates are high and undervalued currency when they are low.

Fuels boom and bust

Under the system of fractional reserve banking the total amount of money in circulation is determined by the sum of the everyday lending decisions of individual banks. Quite understandably these are determined by the bank's responsibility to create shareholder value, not by any sense of responsibility for making prudent macro-economic decisions.

This has the unintended consequence of fuelling quasi-cyclical boom and bust. During the boom there is optimism about the future and banks are only too willing to make loans. These increase the money supply, which further fuels the boom. It also leads to inflation in consumer prices and to inflation in the price of land and other assets. In the years leading up to 2007 the banks made loans against the rising collateral value of land, increasing the money supply and stoking up an unsustainable boom in land prices.

During the subsequent recession there is gloom about future prospects which leads the banks to make fewer loans, the money supply contracts, and recession is exacerbated. In 2009 – 2011 we saw business leaders and government exhorting the banks to lend more to small businesses at a time when the banks, very prudently, were rebuilding their reserves. The money supply created by the banks has been insufficient to keep the economy going, and the Bank of England has had to create money directly itself using the mechanism of Quantitative Easing.

During neither the upswing nor the downswing of the economy has the interest of the economy as a whole been aligned with the self-interest of the banks. Indeed, as sentiment lags behind market fundamentals, almost all actions serve to amplify boom and bust.

Diverts investment into property

Banks can reduce their risks by lending against the collateral value of assets, and they favour landed property over capital assets that have a shorter life. This availability of credit for the purchase of land pushes up property prices and directs investment away from productive enterprise, particularly from small businesses and start-ups.

Subsidises the banks

The fractional reserve banking system gifts to retail and commercial banks a special profit amounting to the interest paid on the credit they create, which Joseph Huber and James Robertson estimated to be over £23 billion per year in the UK in 1998 (2000: 81).

Increases the risk of bank failure

Under the fractional reserve system, banks lend not just the money deposited with them but the much larger amounts of new money that they create. This leverage amplifies the risk to these banks as well as their profits.

Creates and requires indebtedness

Under the fractional reserve system all money other than notes and coin is created as debt. The only way that the money supply can expand is if individuals, businesses and the state take on more and more debt. At an individual level the interest payments required by this debt reduces disposable income and may lead to personal tragedies. At a societal level it reduces spending in the real (non-financial) economy and leads to a progressive transfer of wealth by payment of interest – from poor to rich, from young to old, from manufacturing and commercial sectors to the financial sector, and in the UK from the North to the South.

In summary: the way in which money is introduced into the economy through the fractional reserve system has arisen over the course of time. It no longer serves us well, and fortunately an alternative is readily available. But, as with land ownership, it is we, the electorate, that choose to retain a system that guarantees our own impoverishment.

Stewardship economy

In a stewardship economy a franchise is never gifted to business interests. A monopoly or oligopoly may be most appropriately managed by the private sector, but even if the banks were judged to be particularly effective in the role of issuing new money then banking franchises to issue money as interest-bearing debt should be auctioned at regular intervals and we should all benefit from the revenue.

The banks, however, failed us spectacularly in the years leading up to 2007 by creating too much money and inflating a boom in land prices and there is no reason why their dispersed lending decisions should lead to them issuing the right amount of money for the economy to function well. In spite of the understandable reluctance most people have to allowing the state to 'print' money it should at least have the wellbeing of the economy as its goal and be democratically accountable. The state has access to a mechanism that it currently fails to use that would both give it more direct macroeconomic control and generate some of its own revenue – full reserve banking.

Full reserve banking

Full reserve banking is an example of monetary reform that is similar in spirit to the proposals of Irving Fischer (1936), Milton Friedman (1960) and James Tobin (1987). It has been advocated by many authors over recent decades, particularly Joseph Huber and James Robertson in *Creating new money* (2000) and in a joint submission to the Independent Commission on Banking by a collaboration between Richard Werner, the New Economics Foundation and Positive Money (Richard Werner et al 2011).

The essence of this proposal is that the state terminates the banks' franchise to create new money under the fractional reserve system. This applies to the creation of sterling by all banks, wherever they are domiciled. At the same time the state grants to the Bank of England the right to create money, in digital form, 'out of thin air' – just as the retail banks do now and just as it has been doing since 2009 in its programme of quantitative easing. (The difference is that the money created for quantitative easing is not used to finance the government or its debt directly, but to buy government bonds from financial institutions. It is thus described purely as an instrument of monetary policy, though its main function has been to support these institutions.)

When the central bank judges that the money supply needs to expand it would create money by writing it, interest-free, into the transaction account that the government holds with it. When it judges that the money supply needs to contract, it would deduct money from this government account.

The government would be responsible for deciding how to spend new money into circulation, and how to live within its reduced means when money is taken from its account.

Advantages of full reserve banking

The most significant advantage of full reserve banking is that it removes the risk of bank failures and taxpayer bailouts. There are many additional advantages including direct control by the Bank of England over the money supply, interest rates set in the market, counteracting boom and bust, a transfer of the financial benefits of issuing money from the banks to the state and providing a medium of exchange without requiring anyone to go into debt.

Direct control of the money supply by the central bank

With full reserve banking, as with fractional reserve banking, the Bank of England and its monetary policy committee is responsible for the control of the money supply. Just as in an ownership economy, it aims to meet an inflation target set by government when deciding whether to expand or contract the money supply. But instead of intervening indirectly by influencing interest rates it directly determines the amount of money in circulation and so can in principle provide a more stable money supply.

Interest rates set in the market

Under full reserve banking, interest rates reflect the balance of supply and demand for credit and find their own level in the marketplace. They are no longer underpinned by the base rate set by the monetary policy committee and the open market transactions of the central bank.

Interest rates, exchange rates and discount rates would be undistorted and lower.

Counteracting boom and bust

Full reserve banking ensures that the money supply is more stable, unaffected by the banks' willingness to lend and borrowers' willingness to go into debt. The Bank of England can take counter-cyclical action directly by increasing the money supply in recession and reducing it during the upswing.

The state and its citizens are the beneficiaries

During transition from fractional reserve banking, each time a borrower redeems a bank loan that was created under the regime of fractional reserve banking the money supply contracts. To meet the needs of the economy, the central bank would create new money to balance that destroyed by the redemption, by writing it in to the government's transaction account.

The state benefits by the difference between the face value of the new money and the cost of creating it, known as seigniorage. In addition to its existing seigniorage from issuing notes and coin, the government could have anticipated an annual income of around £49 billion in 1998, nearly 15 per cent of its annual tax revenue (Joseph Huber & James Robertson 2000: 84).

If the government then managed to live within its means (the revenue it derives from stewardship fees) it would be free from the need to borrow money on the bond markets, and the government would no longer be beholden to 'the markets'.

Indebtedness

The money supply does not require indebtedness by individuals, businesses or the state. We could all, if we chose to, reduce or eliminate our debt without wrecking the economy.

All borrowers, including the government, would benefit from a reduction in interest payments on their loans which would feed through into reduced costs of production and lower consumer prices. Assuming an interest rate of 5 per cent this would amount to a £75 billion saving each year (James Robertson 2012: 17).

Local currencies

In addition to national currencies, we need local currencies that support local economies and not do not leak away further afield. A local currency make it possible for the amount of money in local circulation to be determined by local institutions.

International monetary reform

Money is an essential requirement for international trade. At present the U.S. dollar functions as the main international 'reserve currency', though as the U.S' financial dominance wanes it is complemented by a competing range of currencies including the euro, yen, rouble and increasingly the yuan. This situation, in which a small number of countries receive a subsidy to create money for international use, directly parallels the national arrangements by which a small number of banks create money for national use and benefit from the interest paid on this debt. James Robertson estimates that the world pays the U.S over $400 billion a year for using the dollar as the main global currency (James Robertson 2009: 6).

Robertson's proposal for international monetary reform mirrors the proposal for national reform. A new international currency should be established by a world monetary authority and issued by writing it into an account of the United Nations, which in turn puts it into circulation by spending for global public purposes (James Robertson 2009:6).

Cryptocurrencies

The options for creating a currency have expanded in recent years since the invention of Bitcoin, driven by the wish for a currency that is not under the control of a state or central bank and not susceptible to deliberately engineered inflation. As currencies are essentially records in electronic ledgers, the challenge was to introduce a ledger to replace those of the banks. Rather than introduce a central ledger, with the risks of loss of data and corruption this would entail, the fictional inventor of Bitcoin developed a decentralised database that is based on blockchain technology. Many blockchain-based cryptocurrencies are in circulation, but they are not legal tender and serve mainly as speculative assets. The underlying technology may become the basis for state-backed currencies.

Banking

Full reserve banking is not just a mechanism for giving the central bank greater control over the money supply or for increasing government revenue. Its main purpose is to remove the risk of bank failures and the associated risk of banks needing taxpayer bailouts.

Ownership economy

Banking functions

The core functions of banking are to make loans, take deposits and administer payments. Banks may also provide a variety of additional financial services including buying and selling assets for their customers on commission, and trading on their own behalf.

It is unusual for an entrepreneur to have the resources necessary to develop their idea into a profitable business, so bankers play a vital role in making finance available. There are records dating back to 2000 BCE of merchants making loans to traders who transported goods between cities. A merchant or banker might use their own wealth to fund a venture, or they might act as intermediaries, taking deposits from people who want a share of the profits and accept a share of the risk.

In the mid–20th century it was sometimes said that banking was governed by the 3-4-5 rule – take deposits at 3 per cent, make loans at 4 per cent and get on the golf course by 5 o'clock. Golf in this aphorism is a metaphor for the personal relationships that lenders had with borrowers, enabling them to make judgements about whether the borrower was likely to be able to repay the loan from a future stream of income.

When a bank lends money it is exposed to solvency risk, the risk that the value of its assets falls below the value of its liabilities – for example because of business failures leading to defaults on loans. Solvency risk can only be minimised if banks make prudent lending decisions.

When a bank lends money that is held on deposit it is also exposed to liquidity risk because its 'assets' (the loans that it has made) are not as liquid as its liabilities (the deposits, which it may have to repay to customers). Liquidity risk occurs whenever a bank borrows 'short' (promising to repay depositors on demand) and lends 'long' (committing its loans for months or years). Even when it is solvent it can find itself subject to a bank run and unable to repay its depositors. Such a run may be prevented if there is a credible deposit guarantee scheme, although this needs to be very well financed in situations where there are simultaneous risks to many institutions.

As pointed out above, this account of banks lending the money deposited with them is, of course, these days a fiction. Under the fractional reserve system, they make loans that are many times greater than their deposits simply by writing the credit in to customers' accounts. This leverage greatly magnifies both the liquidity and the solvency risks.

Banks serve another essential role in the economy by providing a payment system. Having accepted money in the form of deposits they move it electronically between accounts, making it possible for transactions to take place safely, securely and speedily.

Banks provide important financial services for clients, such as underwriting share issues and brokering. And they may trade on their own behalf in shares, options, derivatives and so on (proprietary trading).

Types of bank

Retail banks (which provide services to individuals and to small and medium-sized enterprises) and commercial banks (which provide these services to large companies) each combine within a single institution the functions of loan-making, deposit-taking and administration of payments.

Investment banks conduct business on commission and on their own behalf. There are synergies between the functions of retail and commercial banking and those of investment banking. These include diversification and the provision of a full range of financial services to their clients. But where banks are operating the fractional reserve system there are several reasons for advocating the separation of banking functions. These include the potential conflicts of interest between the functions (of which the LIBOR rate fixing scandal is just one example), the inappropriate mixing of the appropriately risk-taking investment bank culture with the appropriately risk-averse lending function and the danger that the failure of high-risk activities brings down the lower-risk functions. The Glass-Steagall Act was put into place in the U.S in 1933 after the collapse of a large part of the American retail and commercial banking system in that year; the Act required the separation of investment banking from retail and commercial banking. The repeal of the Act in 1999 by Bill Clinton is one of the factors that contributed to the credit crunch of 2007.

The bank failures of 2007–2008

One way in which banks have sought to counter the risk of default by other financial institutions has been to insure themselves by means of Credit Default Swaps. These were traded extensively, particularly by investment banks.

Another way to counter the risk has been for banks to sell risky loans on to third parties. Loans were bundled and sliced into tranches with different levels of risk – the infamous Collateralised Debt Obligations. The risky tranches carried high interest rates, appealing to investors looking for high returns and willing to accept high risks. But, at a distance from the original lender, it proved impossible to appreciate how risky they were.

These practices themselves have two problems that became apparent in 2007. One is that the banks and thrifts (building societies) that granted sub-prime mortgages in the U.S had felt able to lend without worrying about whether the loans would be repaid. The other problem was that insurers underestimated the risk that they were insuring, and, when required to pay out, the insurers themselves failed and had to be rescued by the state. Both banks and insurers were operating under conditions of moral hazard.

As in any asset price boom the prices (of houses in this case) eventually peaked, initially in the sub-prime market in the U.S. As borrowers began to default, the insurers became liable to make payments to lenders who had suffered losses. The complexity of the instruments and the extent of trading meant that no one knew the level of exposure of each institution to the risk of default. This meant that no institution could be treated as credit-worthy, resulting in a 'credit crunch'.

The drying-up of interbank lending in turn caused the failure of institutions that were not particularly exposed to sub-prime mortgages but were dependent on short-term borrowing on the interbank market. In the UK the Northern Rock bank had to be taken into public ownership in September 2007.

The investment bank Lehman Brothers, heavily exposed to losses in the land market, went into bankruptcy in the U.S. in September 2008. The interconnectedness of the global financial system meant that once one institution was in danger of default, all were. Lending on housing was a global business, other countries were poised with their own housing bubbles ready to burst, and the crisis became a global one. Governments and central banks around the world judged that the failure of a single financial institution could trigger the collapse of the global financial system, that the banks were 'too big to fail'.

Jane Jacobs introduced the term 'monstrous hybrid' (1992: 93) to describe what happens when the separate ethical principles that are appropriate for government and for commerce become intermingled. The banking system had become a monstrous hybrid in which the losses were borne by governments and their taxpayers at the end of a long period during which financial institutions had enriched themselves and their senior managers.

Governments stepped in to guarantee the losses of the banks and by April 2009 the cost to the U.S., Eurozone and UK amounted to almost $9 trillion – about $2 trillion in liquidity support, $2.5 trillion in asset purchases including nationalisations and partial nationalisations and $4.5 trillion in guarantees (IMF 2009).

Governments effectively wrote a blank cheque to support the private sector, and this proved too much for the economies of several countries including Iceland, Greece, Ireland and Portugal. In the UK, the bailout of the Royal Bank of Scotland alone took the government of the UK to the brink of financial collapse and the taxpayer has had to provide subsidies and guarantees to banks totalling over £1.2 trillion. If we make the assumption that only half of this is required, it will still amount to ten times the annual school budget, six times the health budget or £10,000 per person in the UK.

The failure of the banking system has, understandably, led to calls for reform. Retail and commercial banking needs to be conducted in a way that minimises risk to depositors, to banks and to the government.

Regulation

The state imposes regulations on the banking system that are designed to mitigate both solvency and liquidity risks. To mitigate solvency risk, it requires banks to hold enough capital reserves to survive any defaults on loans that could reasonably be anticipated. To mitigate liquidity risk, it underwrites the Financial Services Compensation Scheme (deposit insurance).

Moral hazard

The Financial Services Compensation Scheme provides an explicit guarantee to depositors that they will not lose their deposits in a failed bank, up to a current maximum in the UK of £85,000 per person per banking group. This absolves depositors from thinking about whether their bank is taking inappropriate risks.

Even more serious is the implicit guarantee currently provided to banks which believe that, in the event of insolvency, they will be bailed out by the government. In these circumstances it is logical for them to make risky investment decisions, unscrutinised by their customers and knowing that they will retain any gains that they make while the state will bear any losses. This constitutes what is known as 'moral hazard'.

Collateral

The purpose of healthy business borrowing is to enable a business to meet the whole of its costs of production, capital and revenue, until it generates a profit. When a bank lends money, it may safeguard this investment in a number of ways. Most importantly it needs to satisfy itself that the enterprise is financially viable and will be able to repay both interest and capital from its profits. In addition, it may ask the borrower for security, or collateral. The form of security most frequently requested, and given, is a first charge on property owned by the enterprise – much of the value of which may lie in land rather than improvements.

Banks have frequently made the mistake of paying more attention to collateral (security) than to profitability. This has led them to lend to enterprises that are not viable but have not been adequately investigated because of their ability to offer land as collateral. The focus on collateral also discourages banks from lending to viable and worthwhile enterprises that are not landowners.

Banking and house prices

The price of property depends on the interplay of supply and demand – demand in the economic sense of a desire to acquire something backed by the ability to pay for it. Most homeowners do not have enough cash to buy a home and are only able to do so by borrowing from a bank or building society.

The willingness of banks and building societies to engage in mortgage lending therefore increases demand for property and pushes up house prices. The maximum amount that the bank will lend is determined by the borrower's ability to repay the loan and the value of the property – as estimated by a valuer. During times of rapid house price increases, banks play a role in inflating the housing bubble by lending ever higher multiples of earnings while requiring smaller deposits and may even accept valuations that are based on an expectation of continuing price increases rather than current values.

Although trading in complex financial instruments was the trigger for the credit crunch, its underlying cause was the familiar quasi-cyclical behaviour of the housing market, fuelled by the expansion of credit. Unwise bank lending against the collateral of over-valued land has been the root cause of bank failures for hundreds of years and around the world.

Proposals for banking reform

The Independent Commission on Banking (2011) set out the main options for reform of the banking system (though it failed to give any consideration to monetary reform). These options included a variety of proposals for each of the following:

o   separating deposit-taking from risky activities (e.g., the separation of retail and commercial from investment banking along the lines of the Glass-Steagall Act)

o   mechanisms that would enable this separation to take place rapidly in times of financial crisis (e.g., 'living wills')

o   increasing banks' capital and liquidity requirements ('Basel III')

o   rapid recapitalisation – provision for the debt owed by banks (bonds) to be automatically converted into shares (equity) if a bank's capital falls below a certain level (e.g., 'bail-in' and 'contingent capital').

Identifying and implementing appropriate reform is a challenging task, particularly in the context of extraordinarily powerful banks that are internationally mobile. However, governments do not have the resources to bail out banks using taxpayers' money in the future, so as a safety net underlying any possible reform, it is essential that mechanisms for rapid recapitalisation are in place and that share-holders in a bank understand that they will bear the full cost of any losses. The Bank of England can no longer act as 'lender of last resort'.

In summary: In 2007-2008 banks failed to serve the interests of their depositors, investors, themselves or the economy as a whole. After profiting for decades from the subsidy granted by their franchise to create money, they successfully externalised the risks associated with their activities and states and their taxpayers had to meet the costs. This was not a case of a 'few bad apples' or of an arrogant banking culture but of a design failure of the entire banking system. The Independent Commission on Banking fiddled with the details of the banking system but failed even to consider the radical change to full reserve banking that would generate safety for taxpayers and remove the subsidy we provide through fractional reserve banking.

The whole economy depends on the ability of banks to take deposits and handle payments safely, functions that should be invulnerable except to bank robbers and fraudsters. These functions need to be insulated from the risks that are inherent in the loan-making and trading functions of banking.

This focus on bank failures, however, should not distract us from the even more damaging effect of bank lending for the purchase of assets like land. It is here that the fractional reserve system amplifies the economy's natural oscillations between boom and bust.

Stewardship economy

The bank failures of 2007–2008 are likely to be interpreted and remembered as being caused by a 'credit crunch' brought on by an appetite for risk and trading in poorly understood derivatives. This focus on banking, however, allows us to ignore what underlies this set of banking failures and recession: the collapse of a property price bubble. This is a common cause of banking failures, for example the U.S.savings and loan crisis of the 1980s, the Japanese banking failures and recession of the 1990s and the nationalisation of the Swedish banking system in 1992. Stewardship offers a certain way of avoiding any future property price bubbles by stabilising the price of land – though it offers no protection from bubbles in any other sorts of assets.

In addition to reforming property rights to land and the consequent stabilisation of land values, a stewardship economy would ideally see parallel reforms to money supply (full reserve banking) and to other government-granted monopoly rights such as intellectual property rights. Banks would be safer by operating full reserve banking.

Separating banking functions

The joint submission to the Independent Commission on Banking by Richard Werner, the New Economics Foundation and Positive Money (Richard Werner et al 2011) proposed that banks should be required to keep safe the money that depositors want kept safe, and to invest money that they want invested. It would do so by classifying all bank accounts as either transaction accounts or investment accounts.

In this proposal for full reserve banking, transaction accounts replace current accounts as the mechanism by which payments are made. When a customer makes a deposit into a transaction account, the bank transfers the whole amount to its own transaction account at the Bank of England. Money in transaction accounts is held off balance sheet in fiduciary trust and is available only for making payments not for investment. A bank, even if it became bankrupt, would still be able to repay in full, and more-or-less instantly, all those who had made deposits into its transaction accounts as the resources to do so would be held by the Bank of England.

Deprived of the substantial subsidy provided by fractional reserve banking, banks would need to charge their customers for operating transaction accounts. Charges would be minimised by increased competition among banks in the provision of transaction accounts. Traditional building societies, credit unions, mutuals and Community Development Finance Institutions would find themselves on a level playing field with banks when offering transaction accounts. They would also have much lower entry costs than under fractional reserve banking as they would require minimal regulatory oversight and no great capital reserves.

There would be no need for a state-backed deposit guarantee scheme and no limit on the amount that could be safely deposited in such an account, as all deposits are safe. Deposits in transaction accounts do not earn interest, and anyone seeking interest would instead deposit the money in an investment account.

Deposits in investment accounts are handled in an entirely different way. The deposits become the property of the bank, and the investment account does not contain money but a record of the amount the bank owes to the depositor. The bank may use the funds deposited in whatever way it likes (for example to fund loans, credit cards, mortgages, investment or trading on its own behalf) subject to the guarantees it offers to depositors in that account. A depositor would not have instant access to the money they deposit but could withdraw it after either a notice period or on a defined maturity date.

Investment accounts offer both reward and risk, and the way in which these risks and rewards are shared between the bank and the depositor is made explicit in the guarantees that the bank offers to depositors in that account. These might include a guarantee to repay at least a minimum percentage of the amount deposited and a guarantee of the rate of interest that will be paid. Investors who want a higher rate of return would understand that they bear more of the risk themselves.

Full reserve banking provides for separation of banking functions without the need to break up the banks themselves. If the bank fails, its guarantees are not underwritten by the state but by its shareholders and bondholders.

Under full reserve banking retail and commercial banks, like everyone else apart from the central bank, are banned from creating legal tender.

Regulation

Bank regulation under full reserve banking would largely be limited to the prevention of fraud and misleading advertising, as self-regulation would be designed into all banking functions by the requirement for the full reserve.

As deposits in transaction accounts are fully backed by reserves held with the central bank, they pose no risk to banks or depositors in these accounts, so the state does not need to specify reserve ratios (which are effectively 100 per cent) or to provide deposit insurance. The only necessary regulation of transaction accounts is to carry out checks that banks are not fraudulently failing to transfer deposits to their transaction accounts at the Bank of England.

The profits banks make from lending would come from the difference between the rate of interest charged on loans and that paid to investors. The notice period or maturity date for deposits in investment accounts, combined with limited repayment guarantees, would provide banks with substantial insulation from the risks of a run on the bank by anxious investors.

Losses from investments would put at risk neither the transaction system nor depositors' funds held in transaction accounts. Poorly managed financial institutions could be allowed to fail like any other business. This would have the beneficial effect of imposing market discipline and eliminating moral hazard as well as protecting the state and its taxpayers from risk. The risk to banks, and all financial institutions no matter how big, would be borne by their shareholders, bondholders and in part by the depositors in their investment accounts.

Depositors in investment accounts would, in the event of insolvency, become creditors of the bank and hope to recover some of their investment through normal liquidation procedures. The state does not need to underwrite or guarantee deposits in investment accounts.

The state would however provide regulatory oversight of investment accounts by investigating the guarantees that banks make for their investment accounts. It would need to ensure as far as possible that these are realistic, that the bank will be able in all foreseeable circumstances to meet them.

Full reserve banking would allow the removal of the bulk of regulation from the potentially more risky activities of banks and other financial institutions, including proprietary trading. Regulators would need to ensure themselves that financial institutions were not acting fraudulently, for example using pyramid investment schemes such as those popularised by Bernie Madoff. They would also need to ensure that banks make clear to investors the uses to which their money might be put.

International mobility of banks

International banks might fear that their profits would be diminished and could threaten to relocate their operations. However, to explore this concern, it is worth looking at each of the banking functions in a bit more detail.

Deposits and payments - transaction accounts

Competition for transaction accounts would take place on a level playing field, and barriers to entry into this form of banking could be much lower than at present as there would be no requirement for the bank to be well-capitalised or contribute to deposit insurance. Banks would be lightly regulated – all that would be needed is that they would have to be honest. If the big international banks were not interested in providing such accounts at competitive rates, no doubt local institutions like local banks, credit unions and mutuals would be.

Loan-making – investment accounts

If full reserve banking were introduced in the UK, any creation of sterling by banks would be illegal. This would apply whether a bank was located in the UK or abroad. Making loans would still be a profitable business even without the fractional reserve subsidy, and it is unlikely that banks would move abroad just because the UK loans business was less profitable. Banks in the UK operating accounts denominated in dollars, euros, yen or yuan would continue these activities unchanged for as long as other currency jurisdictions permitted it.

Trading

A country adopting full reserve banking would become an attractive location for investment banks and hedge funds. Their activities need to be regulated only very lightly (to prevent fraud) because if they became insolvent they could be allowed to fail just like any other company.

Collateral

As land in a stewardship economy has a zero market rent net of stewardship fees (and so, zero market value), no borrowing or lending is required for the purchase of land.

Bubbles in the price of many assets, including commodities and shares, occur in a stewardship economy as they do in an ownership economy. But bubbles in the price of land, including house prices, simply do not occur. Stewardship economies are not prone to the threats to the banking system that arise from the collapse in the price of homes and commercial properties. As land has no market value, what can be used as collateral for bank loans?

If current banking practice were adopted in a stewardship economy the amount of capital that enterprises could borrow would be more limited than in an ownership economy because land has no market value, and only the improvements could be used as collateral.

In a future stewardship economy, banks will need to rely less on the security of collateral (which, in ownership economies has proved to be illusory when land values fall) and more on close relationships with their borrowers to allow thorough assessments of how much debt the borrower can safely take on. In this there is much that banks can learn from microfinance institutions, which lend to borrowers with no assets to offer as collateral. These are most successful where they are embedded in a community that can itself hold borrowers to account for their repayments.

In a stewardship economy there are a variety of ways for banks to secure their loans:

- Community of borrowers. Some banks and provident societies make loans on the security of personal guarantees. If each individual guarantees only a small sum, the bank lends to enterprises that have a large number of people committed to their success and this reduces the risk of failure.

- Community banking. Here lenders and borrowers live in the same local community and the community can hold borrowers to account for their repayments.

- Islamic finance. Sharia law prohibits a lender from charging interest on a loan. There are other ways in which a lender can benefit from lending, either by charging rent (if the loan is on a property) or by participating in an enterprise on a profit-sharing and loss-sharing basis. Islamic banking puts the focus for investors on identifying enterprises that they think are ethical and viable, not on enterprises which happen to own property that can be held forfeit.

The lack of a market value for land would cause lenders to give greater attention to the capacity of the enterprise for long-term sustainable growth and to its significance to local people, consumers and employees. The apparent problem of lack of collateral provides part of the solution for mitigating the risks of banking and ensuring that it serves the needs of businesses that are sound and enjoy widespread support in their communities.

In summary: In an ownership economy banks have been gifted the franchise for creating money through the fractional reserve system. When money is created in this way consumers, producers and governments go into debt to provide the medium of exchange for commerce. Banks expand the money supply during a boom and contract it in a recession. By lending against the collateral value of land, they fuel an increase in land value and lay themselves open to losses when land values fall.

In a stewardship economy with full reserve banking, money is created directly by the state. This:

o   enables the central bank to stabilise the money supply by taking direct control of the amount of money issued

o   avoids the need for widespread indebtedness

o   removes the costly subsidy provided by governments to banks.

Full reserve banking requires banks to keep safe, in transaction accounts, the deposits that customers want to keep safe and invest the deposits, in investment accounts, that they want to invest. This stabilises banks and makes it possible to remove the deposit insurance scheme and to reduce the level of regulation on banks and other financial institutions. It also avoids the need for government bail-outs and so reduces moral hazard.

Chapter 3 Efficiency in the short term

An economy is effective if it achieves what it is intended to achieve, and efficient when it maximises the ratio of useful outputs to inputs.

As Robert Kuttner (1996) suggests, one might 'intend' that an economy would achieve three broad sorts of objective on different time-scales:

- In the short term, an economy should direct or allocate people, information, capital and land so that they are employed efficiently.

- In the long term, an economy should foster innovation and technological development.

- Over the medium term (say 10–20 years), an economy should display some stability, rather than lurching from times of plenty to times of scarcity.

This chapter focuses on how a stewardship economy allocates economic activity more efficiently than an ownership economy from the (microeconomic) perspective of individual businesses and consumers – by removing taxes that impose a deadweight loss on the economy and by freeing up the market in land and labour.

Ownership economy

Economists are fond of the example of idealised fish markets, where high prices in times of scarcity ensure that fish is allocated to the buyers who are most willing and able to pay; and where, when the catch is abundant, buyers are encouraged to take it off the fishermen's hands by low prices.

In such a market, prices are influenced by the interaction between supply and demand, which is dynamic and complex. In the short term, the traditional economic idea that supply and demand come into momentary balance, or equilibrium, can provide a useful approximation.

Taxes discourage whatever is being taxed, distort the way the whole economy works and reduce overall economic activity – the 'lost surplus'. This impact is described as the 'deadweight loss of taxation' and may amount to around £100 billion each year in the UK.

Inefficient labour market

An efficient labour market is one in which most of those who want to work have the opportunity to do so. There are several factors that make the labour market highly inefficient in ownership economies, particularly the cost to the employer of taxation, employment protection measures and the associated red tape. The benefit system contributes to the inefficiency of the labour market.

The housing market also makes a contribution to this inefficiency by impairing labour mobility. Owner-occupiers and tenants in social housing move home less often than people in market rental accommodation. They are more likely to put up with unsatisfactory work and less likely to move to a more attractive job. This is damaging to the economy – a 10 per cent increase in home ownership rates is associated with a 2 per cent increase in the unemployment rate when comparisons are made either between countries or within one country over the course of time. (Andrew Oswald 1996:16) Owner-occupation and social housing both increase unemployment by reducing labour mobility.

Inefficient market for land

When economists explore the reasons for an ownership economy's poor performance, they often identify inefficiencies and rigidities in the labour and capital markets. They rarely discuss the way in which very real barriers to a free and efficient market in land hold the economy back. These barriers include infrequent exposure of land to the market, incomplete information, transaction costs, speculation and (from time to time) rent controls.

We usually assume that land is being used with maximum (allocative) efficiency when it is under the control of whoever will pay the most for it. For example, in the U.S. the Hawk Mountain Sanctuary Association demonstrated that the most efficient use of a mountain was for hawk conservation – by buying it. But in an ownership economy there is only a weak incentive to sell under-used land so many properties are rarely exposed to the market.

In the UK, significant amounts of land are still held by the descendants of those who received it as a gift from the crown. This has never been allocated by exposure to the market. And although land is generally in the possession of someone who paid the most for it, this payment was made by someone who valued it highly at some time in the past not by whoever currently values it most highly. Land, even where it might once have been allocated to the highest bidder and used optimally, is no longer necessarily well used.

Buyers and sellers cannot inform themselves completely about which properties are currently available on the market, or even about the prices at which other properties have been bought and sold. This causes inefficiencies in the land market.

In an ownership economy it may make sense to leave land idle because charges for buying and selling land (including Stamp Duty Land Tax, legal costs and estate agents' fees) discourage transactions and make the market 'sticky'. Owners are particularly likely to retain underused properties when the land or improvements are unusual or unique.

In addition, Stamp Duty Land Tax thresholds introduce small price distortions. For example, a property marketed for £250,000 will sell for £252,500 including Stamp Duty Land Tax at 1 per cent, while a property marketed for £250,001 will sell for £257,501 including Stamp Duty Land Tax at 3 per cent. This means that people will be willing to make bids for a property up to a threshold but unwilling to bid just above that threshold.

In an efficient market, the market value of land would be equal to the discounted stream of expected revenue, the rent. But in ownership economies there is also a speculative element to land transactions. When the market is rising people anticipate that it will continue to rise and are prepared to pay a bit more – either because as an investor they anticipate a capital gain or because as a householder they believe that it will become increasingly difficult to 'get on the housing ladder'. They may do so even when they are not intending to use the land to the full. When the market is falling, people who are financially overstretched may have no option but to sell, perhaps as a result of repossession by their mortgage lender, and the flood of forced sales depresses market values below what they would otherwise be.

The rental market for commercial and industrial properties is frequently inefficient as the result of upward-only rent reviews. It is understandable that there should be a regular review of the rent that a tenant pays for a property, and that when the market rent of similar properties rises the rent of the index property should be raised as well. But many tenancies contain clauses that prevent the converse from happening. When market rents for similar properties fall, these clauses prevent the rent of the index property from falling. This results in unnecessary financial distress to tenants, the failure of businesses, voids and unoccupied premises.

Ownership economies have, from time to time, responded to the lack of affordable housing for the low-paid by limiting the amount that a landlord can charge a tenant. This reduces the market value of the house (unless the landlord obtains vacant possession which may involve deception and even violence) and reduces the amount of housing available for rental.

Index of land value

If you are looking for information about the functioning of the economy, you don't have far to go to get a fairly clear idea of the stocks and flows of labour and capital. Figures for the rate of unemployment, with regional variations, are published monthly and average rates of pay are available by industry. Rates of interest are updated daily, FTSE share indices provide a continuous measure of the value of publicly quoted companies, and utilisation rates of capital equipment are available. But things are very different for information about land value.

House price indices are compiled by Building Societies like the Nationwide and the Halifax. These are based on recent market transactions, separated into a series of bands and aggregated to provide averages for broad geographical areas. The Land Registry publishes a monthly House Price Index which tracks the price of an average home, based on the sale price of all homes in England and Wales. Unlike the indices complied by estate agents, the House Price Index is adjusted to allow for the proportion of top-end and bottom-end properties that are sold that month.

Each of these indices describe movements in the price of property as a whole - the price of buildings and other improvements as well as land. As the proportion of value attributed to land and to improvements varies according to the type of property, location in the country, historical time and the nature and condition of improvements, it is not possible to use the indices to provide accurate information about the changing value of land.

Each of the indices suffers in addition from its own limitations. Those constructed by the building societies refer only to sales for which the buyer takes out a mortgage with their society, and the value recorded is not the documented sale price. The Land Registry Index is more complete, but the property values used may not reflect the market value, if, for example, the property is transferred by private agreement and the index is published three months in arrears.

The lack of accurate real-time information about land values makes it difficult to make rational decisions about investment in land, as well as hampering attempts to understand and model the workings of the economy as a whole.

Stewardship economy

Avoiding the deadweight loss of taxation

If stewardship fees replace conventional taxes, economic efficiency is improved because there is no deadweight loss of taxation, and this results in an improvement in economic efficiency. This is the central pragmatic reason for advocating stewardship.

Efficient labour market

Stewardship improves the efficiency of the labour market by making employment more affordable, supporting workers during redundancy and encouraging part-time working as well as improving labour mobility and providing lifetime funding for retraining.

In a stewardship economy, more people feel free to rent because home ownership is not an investment decision. This means that they should find it easier to move home to meet their work needs.

Even if someone remains in the same job through their whole working life, they will need education, training and retraining. These are even more important now that most people change jobs at least once during their lifetime or have portfolio careers. Training increases a person's employability and, so, increases the supply of labour. These 'supply-side' measures improve the capabilities of the workforce and, thereby, the economy's flexibility and capacity to develop and innovate. A Universal Income enables each person to take a break from work to train or retrain whenever they need to.

Efficient market for land

Stewardship ensures that land is more often exposed to the market, provides full information about all land, cuts transaction costs, and removes speculative costs.

Land is allocated to the person or firm that is willing to pay the most for it, as in an ownership economy, but there is a crucial difference. The payment is not an investment but an ongoing liability to pay its market rent. Stewardship fees – set at auction and annually updated – ensure that the land is under the control of whoever is currently prepared to pay the most for it. Stewardship supports the appropriate transfer of land to the person or body that values it most highly at that particular time, and so ensures that land is exposed to the market more often than in an ownership economy.

There is a publicly accessible register of all properties, which provides separate valuations of the improvements and of the land. These are up-to-date estimates of market rent. This comprehensive information for buyers and sellers is the essential ingredient of an efficient land market.

There is no tax on transfers and so the land market is less sticky and more efficient.

The stewardship fees reflect the 'fundamental' value of the market rent of the property, undistorted by speculative expectations of future changes in market value. There are no rent controls and none of the associated distortions.

The Land Stewardship Trust uses the figures from its auctions to publish an index of land values that is updated daily and is based on the value of land alone, unsullied by the value of any improvements.

Chapter 4   Long-term growth

Long-term growth looks quite different in ownership and stewardship economies. In an ownership economy it is all-important, the only thing that keeps people out of unemployment, and an essential ingredient in the pursuit of increasing wealth. One of the most important policy questions in an ownership economy is what governments can do to stimulate economic growth, to overcome all the barriers to low growth. Only a minority of people challenge the need for further economic growth in high-consumption economies in spite of the environmental damage that much growth causes.

In a stewardship economy the danger is not too little growth, but too much.   Relieved of the deadweight loss of taxation, a stewardship economy tends to grow faster than an ownership economy. However, stewardship provides ways to prevent firms and consumers from ignoring the impact of their actions on the environment and these measures have the effect of reducing economic growth. And, critically, stewardship provides a way of redistributing wealth, which prevents the damage to the poor that would result if growth slowed in an ownership economy.

Understanding and promoting economic growth

Dependence on economic growth

The main reason why ownership economies cannot manage without economic growth is because income is distributed on the basis of the work that people do or have done, supplemented by income from investments and benefits. Jobs are essential in ownership economies if people are to support themselves without recourse to benefits. As productivity increases through technological advance and investment, it is only possible to maintain current levels of employment if there is economic growth. Full employment, or something close to it, is necessary to ensure that most of the population are included in the economy.

Think of the example of the arms trade. The UK is a major exporter of arms and there have been repeated scandals in our relationships with repressive regimes. But the UK government always provides substantial diplomatic and financial support to the defence industry, for example by shouldering the commercial risk through export credit guarantees. The reason that is given is always the same – British jobs.

Source of long-term growth

Probably the most extraordinary thing about economies, apart from their very existence, is the exponential rate of growth in economic activity (GDP) that most have shown over the last two hundred and fifty years. This is particularly striking by comparison with the previous 10,000 years or so, since the development of settled agriculture. Long-term growth is more significant, though often less obvious at the time, than short-term boom and bust.

Long-term growth requires more than efficiency of allocation in the short term and full employment of labour and capital in the medium term. It depends on improvements in productivity, and therefore on developments in both human capital and technology – which ultimately require investment. It can be better understood by thinking of the economy as a complex adaptive system than as an equilibrium system.

Equilibrium economics

At the start of the industrial revolution, Adam Smith recognised that economic growth is promoted by the division of labour and the development of machinery (technology) (Adam Smith 1776 Volume I Book I Chapter I:12), and that these require investment in capital. But the equilibrium theory of the classical economists does not contain an explanation, within the model, for economic growth.

Joseph Schumpeter (1942) insisted on the importance of the dynamics of an economy. He viewed markets not as idealised fish auctions but as situations in which sellers differentiate their products and compete on quality or brand more than on price, enabling them to make greater profits and so to invest in innovation and the development of new technologies. Long-term growth requires some slack in the system – high levels of profits and a long-term view are what are needed for investment in new technology, not efficiency that forces prices down and maximises short-term shareholder value. Schumpeter's entrepreneur plays a heroic role in disrupting market equilibrium, but this disruption could not be incorporated into the economic models of his time.

In the 1950s Robert Solow (1958) developed the neoclassical model of growth, in which investment in capital leads to increased productivity. In this model an increase in per capita investment (as a proportion of GDP) shifts output from one equilibrium level of output to a higher equilibrium level of output. This does not explain sustained economic growth until technological progress is introduced as an additional, exogenous, factor. Technology leads to greater productivity; and so, in a virtuous circle, to more savings, investment and yet another round of technological development.

In the 1980s Paul Romer (1986)brought this technological driver inside the neoclassical model in what has come to be known as endogenous growth theory. The key to growth in this model is that output reflects not the decreasing returns to physical production, which is the basis of equilibrium economics, but the increasing returns attributed to 'network effects' – like the increasing value of having a telephone as more subscribers are connected, or, more importantly, the increasing return to knowledge as each development 'stands on the shoulders' of the previous sum of knowledge.

Here is an economic model with a positive feedback loop that is capable of explaining and describing sustained exponential growth. And positive feedback is the sort of interaction between the parts of an economic system that leads to complex dynamics not to equilibrium.

Complexity economics

A system is a whole that can also be thought of as a set of interconnected parts, and systems can be characterised as simple or complex. In a simple system – for example, a lever – a change in one element results in a predictable change in other elements. Simple systems move towards states that are either static (at equilibrium) or periodic (regularly repeating themselves) (Capra 1996:130).

Simple does not mean simplistic – simple systems can be very complicated. The clockwork automata of the eighteenth century were no more than machines but seemed so startlingly lifelike that there was speculation as to whether they might indeed be alive. But complicated is not the same as complex.

In complex systems, the behaviour of the interconnected whole cannot be predicted solely from an understanding of the parts. Cause and effect are linked through non-linear processes, including multiple feedback loops – both positive and negative. In such a system even slightly different initial conditions (for example, the tone of voice used to communicate certain words, the sea temperature in the Antarctic or a butterfly flapping its wings in the rainforest) may give rise to wildly different and unpredictable outcomes (for example different weather patterns or emotional states). There is no clear connection between cause and effect.

One of the key features of complex dynamic systems is that their behaviour plays out over time. In John Sterman's Beer Game, (Eric Beinhoker 2005: 168) participants fulfil orders in a simple supply chain. Modest delays in the transmission of orders, combined with very human over-reaction to a developing situation, generate big fluctuations in inventories. These exhibit not-quite regular, not-quite-random behaviour that mimics the quasi-cyclical behaviour of the stock market and of overall economic activity.

It is possible to model these behaviours, and the resulting system-wide behaviour, in several ways. John Sterman (1992) developed the Beer Game as a way to introduce people to System Dynamics. A complementary form of computer simulation is agent-based modelling, in which purposeful software 'agents' interact in the model using behavioural 'rules of thumb' that may change over the course of time. When applied to the economy, this approach goes by many names, perhaps most recognisably 'complexity economics'. (Beinhocker 2007:19)

In the 1990s, Brian Arthur and John Holland (Arthur 2014) led a group that developed an agent-based model, the Santa Fe Institute Artificial Stock Market. Agents were given three pieces of information – the history of the price of the stock, the history of its dividend payments and the risk-free interest rate. Each agent used its own rule of thumb for trading, and the rules evolved over time. The market as a whole showed complex dynamics that are very similar to those of real markets – spells of periodic and quasi-periodic behaviour, spells of tranquillity and stability and spells of stormy and unpredictable behaviour – with quite sudden transitions between them. There are times of growth, which may be exponential, and times of collapse. There is no equilibrium in such systems, and no need to look for external factors when seeking for the cause of dynamic behaviour. Growth, and volatility, are intrinsic to complex economies and are the dynamic consequence of the agents' decision rules, not of external (exogenous) shocks and randomness.

Intervening in complex evolving systems

If you think of the economy as an equilibrium system you will intervene by using short-term interventions which you expect to have predictable consequences. If you think of it as a complex, dynamic, evolving system (Beinhocker 2005) you bring a radical new perspective and might seek to manage the economy and intervene to promote growth by one of the following interventions: introducing perturbations, promoting evolutionary change, developing future orientation and a co-operative culture, shaping the forces of selection and amplification and reshaping institutional arrangements.

Introducing perturbations

Over a short timescale a complex system may demonstrate fairly simple behaviours and be moderately predictable – like tomorrow's weather. A central bank may have some confidence about the impact of an increase in interest rates. But attempts to intervene in a complex system are more fruitfully thought of as the introduction of perturbations whose impact may be broadly anticipated but can never be predicted in detail.

Governments can, and must, intervene in economies; but from the perspective of complexity economics, they need to do so with humility, recognise that they are experimenting, collect feedback and be prepared to learn and change course.

Promoting evolutionary change

The three essential processes in an evolutionary system are the generation of diversity, selection and amplification. Eric Beinhocker (2005:423) points out that these are functions for which markets are particularly well suited. Individuals and firms generate a wide variety of business plans. Some of these are selected by their appeal to consumers and the successful are rewarded, causing these business plans to spread while the less successful fail. This suggests that one element of promoting economic growth is to foster markets in which enterprises can flourish or die.

Future orientation and co-operative culture

It appears that an economy's capacity for growth is related to the behavioural rules or cultural norms of its members (Eric Beinhocker 2005:429). These include norms for individual behaviour (e.g., the work ethic, an internal locus of control, realistic optimism); co-operation (e.g., valuing generosity and fairness but punishing free riders); and innovation (e.g., using the scientific method, valuing dissent and experimentation, celebrating success). Cultures that give attention to the future – supporting behavioural rules of hard work, co-operation and innovation – seem to be particularly prone to economic growth.

Trust is an emergent property of the interactions between individuals, each of whom is using some set of behavioural rules. In a more equal society, whether the comparisons are between countries or between states in the U.S., behaviour is more trusting and co-operative than in an unequal society.

Shaping the forces of selection and amplification

If a government introduces charges for the use of fossil fuels, for example, it is reshaping the economic landscape. This change causes market forces to exert a selection pressure in favour of business plans that use less energy or generate renewable energy, and to reward those who do so.

Reshaping institutional arrangements

Markets and economic growth depend on the integrity of a wide range of key institutional arrangements – the rule of law, absence of corruption, enforceable property rights and so on. Market-based economies are highly dependent on institutional arrangements such as the limited liability company, bankruptcy law, and trusts that allow assets to 'own themselves' (Larry Elliot & Dan Atkinson 2008:287). Governments need to ensure that costs and benefits are not externalised by firms but that these are brought into the firm's accounts, ensuring that prices reflect true costs Changing the rules of underlying institutional arrangements has profound implications for how market mechanisms play out. Stewardship reshapes one of these key institutional arrangements, the system of property rights in the natural world. This is a powerful and appropriate way to intervene in a complex dynamic system.

Growth: Ownership economy

The success of an economy is judged crudely by its rate of growth. This is a poor measure of what is desirable in an economy as, for example, the costs of clearing up an oil spill or mitigating climate change both contribute to growth.

Barriers to growth

Economic growth is often damaging to the environment and fundamentally unsustainable. There are, however, times when an economy needs to grow. And here we find that there are many barriers to growth in ownership economies, most importantly the deadweight loss of taxation (particularly on labour, profits and sales), the inefficient allocation and use of land, and the over-investment in land with accompanying indebtedness. If we could overcome these barriers, our economies would grow faster. But there are other factors necessary for long-term growth including investment and consumer demand.

Investment and savings

Investment plays a key role in the development of technology. It may be provided by people investing in their own small businesses, venture capitalists investing in start-ups and turn-arounds, banks using the savings of their depositors and the money they themselves create or investors in the shares and bonds of firms.

In ownership economies it is common for households to take on debt to buy a home. The risk for this household is that house prices will fall, and the household left with negative equity. The problem for the economy as a whole is that those households that are in a position to invest choose to put their money into land, starving productive enterprise of investment capital. And this propensity to invest in land rather than production is shared by banks and institutional investors who invest directly in property and, even when ostensibly lending to enterprise, make their loans against the collateral of land.

Household debt as a proportion of income has risen over the last 50 years as credit has been made more widely available. It was often said that this increased debt was balanced by the increased value of the assets that people hold. Where these assets are stocks and shares their market valuation is, at least in theory, a measure of their claim on the real productive potential of the economy. Increases in house prices, except those due to new building or substantial refurbishments, do not represent an increase in real assets but the scarcity of homes.

In an ownership economy, levels of debt are not balanced by assets to the extent that is widely assumed, as people discover when house prices fall, and they find that they have negative equity.

Investing in land offers the potential reward of both income and capital gain as the market value of land rises over time. In addition, the tax system deliberately encourages investment in land – for example people's homes are exempt from Capital Gains Tax, and the interest paid on the purchase of buy-to-let properties was an expense allowable against Income Tax until 2020.

Most people in the UK 'invest' far more of their wealth in their home (indeed many borrow heavily to do so) than in stocks and shares. And many choose to invest savings in a holiday home, buy-to-let property or an instrument that reflects land prices. Investment in land reduces the amount that people have available for investment in productive assets, and so reduces the possible production of new wealth.

Is economic growth desirable?

Having established that ownership economies are not well designed for economic growth because of the incentives to invest in land, and before going on to show how much better the prospects for medium-term growth could be in a stewardship economy, we need to question whether economic growth is desirable.

In low-consumption economies, health and life expectancy improve as average income (per capita GDP) rises and people have better access to food, clean water and sanitation. In these economies economic growth is clearly desirable when it lifts people out of absolute poverty, although the benefits may be undermined by the unequal distribution of wealth and by corruption.

In high-consumption economies the orthodoxy is that, here too, economic growth is necessary and desirable. Most people agree that negative economic growth is painful, while positive economic growth papers over the cracks of an economic system in which poverty and unemployment are endemic. But the reason we need economic growth is not to promote health and happiness but to maintain full employment, as it is through employment that we have chosen to share the output of our complex economy.

Happiness, health and life expectancy

In high-consumption economies, increasing levels of average income are not associated with any improvement in average levels of health, happiness or life expectancy (National Research University Higher School of Economics 2018). At the individual level, of course, most people want a higher level of income, as the wealthiest in any country enjoy the best quality of life. However, quality of life depends on relative, not absolute, wealth. The purpose of increasing consumption in high-consumption economies is to compete for social status, and so for well-being. If we want to improve the overall quality of life in high-consumption economies, we are most likely to be successful if we reduce income inequality and take actions that improve the quality of social relationships.

If economic growth falls, however, this might have a negative effect on health and happiness – not because of a drying-up of supposed 'trickle-down' but because our experience of wealth is relative (Economist 12/11/05:115). We compare our present situation with our own past experience. Economic growth makes it easier to tolerate income inequality and its negative impact because we are better off than we used to be, and falling economic growth makes us less tolerant of our positions as we remember that we are worse off than we used to be.

Economic growth and house prices

Economic growth triggers a vicious spiral in which land values rise, people need to earn more to buy (or even rent) a home, and this drives them to work harder and longer, stimulating more economic growth. If parents with young children are to own a home, they now both need to be in work.

For the last 30 years or so people who are concerned about the environment and social justice have been divided between those who oppose and those who advocate economic growth in high-consumption economies. Supporters of growth believe that economic growth is necessary to pay for environmental clean-ups and to improve the living standards of the poor. They point out that environmental standards are higher in wealthier countries. They may accept that the economic system is failing in some key areas like climate change but suggest that growth can continue without undue environmental damage, provided that prices of products reflect the true cost of the environmental damage caused by their production.

They go on to identify the economic growth that is beneficial or neutral to the environment:

- the recycling and renewable energy sectors

- environmental clean-up, like decontamination of polluted sites

- measures to prevent environmental damage

- services that enable people to travel less in their work, like video conferencing

- services that simply transfer tasks that people have previously done for themselves outside the economy, like childcare and making food, into the formal economy.

Opponents of growth point out that exponential growth in living systems is always unsustainable in the long run and in some forms, like cancers, may lead to the death of the organism. They believe that economic growth inevitably brings environmental damage, and that we should aim to halt and even reverse economic growth in high-consumption economies. If we do not, the ecosystem will demonstrate ever more insistently that continuing economic growth is not possible.

Any economy, ownership or stewardship, which reduces the extent of its environmental damage is going to grow more slowly than it has over the last 100 years. The Netherlands Central Bureau of Statistics have estimated that between 1953 and 1989 the 26 per cent of economic activities that are environmentally burdening generated at least 65 per cent of the increase in national income over that time. They estimate that a shift of economic activity from unsustainable to sustainable of 1 per cent would result in a fall in national income of at least 1.5 per cent (Rofie Hueting, Peter Bosch & Bart de Boer 1992:57). This would suggest that a shift to a fully sustainable economy would reduce national income by around 40 per cent.

As a key element of government policy, economic growth did not surface as a means of reducing unemployment until after the second world war and did not become an overarching policy goal until the 1960s (Peter Victor 2008:14). Peter Victor, in his book, 'Managing without growth' (2008:2), argues that growth cannot be sustained and that it has failed to provide high-consumption economies with what it had seemed to promise – full employment, the amelioration of poverty and inequalities, environmental improvement and happiness. He proposes not that we should aim for zero growth, but that we should abandon economic growth as an overriding policy objective, and replace it with more specific economic, social and environmental objectives.

Victor's System Dynamics model of the Canadian economy provides interesting insights into a range of possible future scenarios. A rapid decline in economic growth to zero, with no other changes, leads to steeply rising unemployment, poverty and government debt. However, if this scenario is combined with a reduction in the working week to share out the available work, redistribution of income to eradicate poverty, population stabilisation and investment in health care and education, the result is a reduction in poverty, unemployment and government debt. Similar improvements, combined with a reduction in greenhouse gas emissions, can be obtained even when a tax on energy is added.

These simulations suggest that we could indeed do without economic growth at the same time as reducing greenhouse gas emissions, but that we would have to share out the available income in a radically more equal way.

Consumer behaviour

Consumers are often blamed for their insatiable desires that drive the economy to grow uncontrollably – except when recession prevents them from expressing their desires. And, of course, per capita economic growth would not continue without consumer demand. Ownership economies would not survive without economic growth unless there were to be a significant redistribution of income. Consumers do need to change their individual behaviour, but they will only be able to do so without damaging the economy when we come round to sharing out the fruits of our economy in a way that is more-or-less equal and unrelated to work.

We need to be able to stimulate economic activity when it is wise to do so – for example when recovering from a natural disaster. The insights from complexity economics suggest that the most effective ways of doing so are to promote evolutionary change and reshape institutional arrangements. In the UK, the Treasury and the Bank of England make adjustments to the interest rate and to a whole range of tax exemptions, subsidies and so on. However, while the Treasury makes some attempts to reduce inequalities, it does not do anything to encourage a switch of investment from land to production. And it does not attempt to change the institutional arrangements that underpin the economy such as property rights, company law or the state's relationship with the private sector.

Economic growth requires investment. An economy that permits individual owners to collect the market rent of land and its rising capital value and designs its tax system to discourage production while largely exempting investment in land, does not seem to be designed to stimulate production and growth.

We do need to question the need for economic growth and to be able to do without it when this is the wise course of action. This requires us to find a way of dividing the rewards of the economy that is not so dependent on the amount of work that each of us does.

Growth: Stewardship economy

We are most likely to develop a new relationship with economic growth, one in which we can choose when and how to grow, if we think of the economy as a complex dynamic system. This leads us to pay particular attention to reshaping institutional arrangements, including those based on our fundamental assumptions about property rights.

Investment and savings

Stewardship stimulates growth by reducing household debt and promoting investment in productive activity rather than in holding land. In a stewardship economy when people take out a mortgage to buy a house, they only need to borrow the value of the building, not the value of the land. House prices do not rise or fall because land prices do not rise or fall.

In a stewardship economy people do not treat land as an investment asset. They think of their house as they do a car – as something to be used, or 'consumed'. If they buy a second home it is because they want to use it, not as an investment. This means that savings are more likely to be invested in productive assets, which increases future production.

Choosing whether to grow

A stewardship economy shares some of the wealth created by economic activity with the whole population as Universal Income. This does not directly share the available work, as modelled by Peter Victor, but would serve the same purpose.

People can support themselves, at least partly, with the Universal Income. Full-time employment and full employment are not essential. This means that a stewardship economy has much greater choice about whether to pursue economic growth or not.

There are some areas of the global economy that will need to grow in the future – for example businesses with a low environmental impact and low-consumption economies as a whole. And there are likely to be times in the economic cycle, such as at the onset of the recession of 2008, when there are good arguments for slowing the rate of decline of economic growth. A stewardship economy provides the necessary conditions for such growth where it is needed, because investment is not diverted from production into land and because the absence of conventional taxes, made possible by the collection of stewardship fees, stimulates economic growth.

Environmental charges are intended to reduce environmental damage and will reduce economic growth. One of the great advantages of stewardship is that during transition it is possible to introduce a judicious combination of growth-stimulating tax-replacement with growth-retardant environmental charges.

If stewardship reduces income inequalities, this is likely to promote the sorts of behaviour like co-operation that give rise to innovation, and hence to economic growth.

Some people may choose to earn as much as they can, losing none of these earnings through taxes or withdrawal of benefits; others may choose to live a low-impact lifestyle funded entirely or in part by their Universal Income.

If economic activity falls then the market rent of land will fall, and consequently the level of the Universal Income will fall, too. In response to this reduction in income some people will probably choose to work more, and this will cause a rise in output, market rents and Universal Income.

So, in a stewardship economy a negative feedback mechanism tends to ensure that the overall level of economic activity is maintained at 'appropriate' levels – with 'appropriateness' given its meaning not by the Treasury but by the choices of individuals. Economic growth is determined by the very real work and consumption choices of the people, rather than work and consumption being dictated by the need for economic growth. And this combination of negative and positive feedback produces not equilibrium but dynamic evolving behaviour.

Influencing the economy without controlling it

Stewardship promotes social justice and trust by reshaping institutional arrangements, in particular property rights. This is likely to give rise to long-term economic growth focused on activities that engage the whole population and improve the prospects for the future, through the sustainable use of the environment. Once a stewardship economy is in place there would be a real opportunity for the behavioural rules of individuals to change, particularly those relating to consumption behaviour and work preferences.

The Treasury and the Bank of England would introduce perturbations into the economy when it is not working as they would like, but less frequently than in an ownership economy and without the delusion that they can control the economy as if it were a machine.

In summary: Stewardship is not just some sort of tinkering with the tax-benefit system. One of the most effective ways to change the way a complex dynamic system works is to change its fundamental institutional structure – such as its system of property rights.

In a stewardship economy people borrow less money to buy their homes, so a greater proportion of saving is available for investment in productive assets. This in turn makes possible an increase in future production. Stewardship promotes long-term growth, and reduces the impact of a recession, by providing an institutional framework within which markets flourish without any deadweight loss of taxation. It shapes the forces of selection and amplification by ensuring that prices reflect the true costs of environmental and social damage, thereby reducing both damage to the environment and economic growth. These growth-promoting and growth-retarding impacts may give rise to low, zero or negative rates of growth.

A stewardship economy accommodates to these different rates of growth by sharing the income from production through the Universal Income rather than restricting the beneficiaries to those who have jobs. The rate of economic growth depends not on the desires of the Treasury but on the choices that individuals make about their work-life balance and levels of consumption.

Chapter 5 Boom, bust and inflation

In the medium term, ownership economies lurch from boom to bust. This chapter explores some theories that have been put forward to account for this quasi-cyclical behaviour and concludes that the economy can best be understood as a complex dynamic system in which there are multiple feedback loops and delays. In such a system it is only to be expected that there will be times of stability, times of turbulence and times of quasi-cyclical activity.

The conventional response to these dynamics is to fine-tune monetary and fiscal policy in order to manage demand while avoiding excessive inflation. The opportunities for controlling a complex dynamic system are, however, limited. The most productive approach when a complex system is not behaving as you would like is to change its institutional structures and perturb the cultural norms of its people.

In a stewardship economy a change in one of the institutional structures – the property system – removes one of the factors that contributes to quasi-cyclical activity, boom and bust.

Ownership economy

Boom and bust

There is much data that points to the way in which economic variables change over the course of time. Some of these time series, for example, some form of retail price index, can be tracked year by year for more than 500 years. Others, for example, a stock market index such as the FTSE 100 or the price of a commodity, are available on a minute-by-minute basis over the course of decades.

One of the most important time series is of overall economic activity as measured by per capita GDP. In high-consumption economies this shows an underlying trend of growth over at least the last 250 years and superimposed on this growth there is a pattern of quasi-cyclical change.

At the scale of the economy as a whole this quasi-cyclical behaviour is sometimes described in positive terms as the way that unprofitable enterprises are squeezed out to make way for innovation and development. But prolonged spells when labour and capital are not fully employed are wasteful and destructive. On a smaller scale, individuals, families and communities face the disasters of unemployment, poverty and repossession of their homes.

Business cycles and their possible causes

One way to explore this quasi-cyclical change is to look at the extent to which per capita GDP is correlated with per capita GDP at a later point in time (autocorrelation). Such analysis shows that per capita GDP is highly correlated with what it was a few months ago but not with what it was a few years ago. However, superimposed on this declining correlation there are some peaks – particularly at around 15–20 years and 40–60 years – that indicate quasi-cyclical activity that is not quite regular but also not quite random.

It is possible in these data to recognise the familiar sequence of boom, depression, recession and recovery. These business cycles have been studied intensively, but it has not generally proved possible to predict the peak of any cycle with accuracy – though Fred Harrison (1983 and 2005) has made a good job of predicting the last two 18-year housing cycles in the UK.

Many theories have been developed to explain cyclical behaviour in the economy. Seasonal cycles in agricultural economies are the most intuitively understandable. Most theories attribute cyclical behaviour either to some form of external shock, to fluctuations in aggregate demand or to government activity but a quasi-cyclical pattern is both familiar and intrinsic to complex dynamic systems.

Microeconomic theory looks at the economy from the point of view of a firm, a worker, a consumer. It treats the economy as an equilibrium system, so it looks to external shocks to explain non-equilibrium behaviour such as bubbles, recessions and cycles – 'real business cycle' models. Wars, revolutions, discoveries and migrations have all been proposed. The OPEC oil embargo in 1973–4, for example, led to a fourfold increase in oil prices in 1974 that was rapidly followed by inflation, recession, and severe falls in the stock market and house prices. Attributing quasi-cyclical activity to external shocks suggests that it is not caused by the economy itself. But external shocks are an essentially improbable cause of quasi-cyclical behaviour occurring over hundreds of years, as there is no reason why shocks should occur with any quasi-regularity.

Macroeconomics explores how the economy functions as a whole. It looks for an explanation of its quasi-cyclical behaviour in the internal structure of the economy.

John Maynard Keynes developed his theories in the British economy during a deflationary depression with prolonged high levels of unemployment. He described a downward spiral that can be triggered by nothing more than a loss of consumer confidence – perhaps due to an external factor such as a natural disaster or war, perhaps due to something internal to the economy such as growing unemployment, rising interest rates or simply the expectation of economic contraction (John Maynard Keynes). Consumers lose confidence, borrow less, spend less and hold on to cash. Aggregate demand falls. In response, businesses cut back on investment and eventually shed jobs, feeding back into the downward spiral of falling consumer confidence.

Keynes challenged several of the assumptions of the classical economists. He argued that not all savings are invested, as savers and investors are different people with different motives. He pointed out that prices and wages do not necessarily fall when there are unsold goods and unemployment, as assumed by equilibrium theory. He showed that, even if the economy were to reach equilibrium, it would not necessarily do so at full employment. But his mental model was still that of equilibrium, even though it envisaged movement between equilibrium states.

New Keynesian economists have incorporated into their macro-economic models delays and the less than perfect rationality of economic agents. These represent modifications to, but not an abandonment of, equilibrium economics.

Politicians are quick to claim the credit either for a booming economy or for the elimination of boom and bust, so it is no surprise that the blame for economic cycles is frequently laid at their door. Governments and central bankers use fiscal (taxation and spending) and monetary (money supply and interest rate) policies to counteract the cyclical behaviour of the economy – for example, through the regular review of interest rates by the Bank of England. These policies can backfire if applied inappropriately or at the wrong time – stabilising feedback mechanisms become destabilising if there is a greater delay in their operation than expected, for example. Political theories of the business cycle go further than this and suggest that politicians deliberately manipulate monetary and fiscal policy for electoral reasons. It is in response to these allegations that governments have given central banks an independent role.

While governments may contribute to the business cycle, they cannot be the sole – or even main – cause. Recessions and inflation have recurred for at least the last 500 years, long antedating any attempts of governments to mitigate or manipulate them (Beinhocker 2005:161, Kennedy 1987).

The perspective of complexity economics allows us to relax the need to find a simple cause and effect relationship to explain the quasi-cyclical nature of economic performance, because this sort of behaviour is exactly what you would expect from a complex dynamic system with a diversity of agents interacting to create feedback loops with delays. This understanding liberates us simply to recognise the patterns of boom and bust and explore what is going on, without feeling that we should be able to predict the timing of an economic downturn. That is how we experience complex systems – we know, for example, that we can't predict the quantity and timing of rainfall in a month's time.

Complexity economics leads us to construct dynamic (non-equilibrium) agent-based computer simulations. These require an understanding of the way in which agents – participants in the economy – actually make decisions. They provide a way to explore the way in which these individual behaviours cause markets and the economy to exhibit complex dynamics.

The experience of living through an economic cycle is of waves of optimism and pessimism. These psychological states are not merely the by-products of the economic cycle but contribute to its causation. Consumers' confidence and their propensity to save, invest, and to buy and sell property all affect the economy.

Asset price bubbles

So, what does it feel like to be on the rollercoaster of trading in capital assets, whether these are stocks, shares, commodities or land?

There is no shortage of examples of the rapid collapse of asset prices – Dutch tulip mania in 1637, the South Sea Bubble of 1720, canals in the 1790s, the railway manias of 1847 and 1866, the Wall Street crash of 1929, the dot-com bubble in 2001 and the property markets of the years leading up to 2007 are just some of the most memorable.   Cryptocurrencies may provide a contemporary example.

What all these examples have in common is that the price of an asset was rising, and everyone wanted a slice of it. Sometimes, as with the tulips, this was pure speculation – 'The purchase of an asset in the hope that its price will rise'.   At other times, it could perhaps have been described as investment – 'The purchase of an asset with the intention that it will produce income or capital gain' – where the investor believed they had acquired an interest in an income-generating venture.

During the boom in dot.com shares, there were many people who genuinely believed that the internet had ushered in a new economic order and that the prices of dot.com shares reflected a potential income stream from these new ventures. In retrospect, we can see that they were 'fooled by randomness' (Nassim Taleb 2007) – the pattern of rising values was, in fact, a short-term fluctuation that was heading for a correction. But even an investor who correctly anticipated that the value of shares would continue rising for a little longer, and then fall to zero, would have had a perfectly logical reason for buying shares as long as they believed that they would be able to judge when to sell up before the crash occurred. Exuberance might be irrational, but well-informed speculation can be entirely rational behaviour. It is risky, and some individuals and institutions inevitably lose out when the bubble bursts.

House prices

The 'fundamental' market value of a house, its price based solely on its utility, can be thought of as the capitalisation of future expected rents. This capitalisation is the sum of money you would have to invest today to provide you with a future income stream equal to those rents.

As market rents rise over the long term, the fundamental market value of a home rises. But, superimposed on this trend, there are times of rapid increase followed by times when house prices stagnate or fall.

The decision to buy a house is based on an entirely different set of considerations from the decision to invest in stocks and shares, but there are important parallels. Waves of optimism and pessimism build and deflate bubbles in the housing market exactly as they do in the stock market. During an upturn in the economy there is growing confidence amongst consumers and businesses. Owners of appreciating assets feel wealthier, and this leads them to borrow more and spend more. More homes and businesses are built and refurbished, stimulating demand for household goods and furnishings. As the economy prospers there is greater competition for homes. As house prices rise, it is tempting to use one's home as a cash machine and to borrow against its rising value to finance current spending, investment or speculation. Developers plan buildings that will produce a glut when they are ready for occupation. As speculation develops, banks and building societies lend ever-larger sums of money against ever more optimistic valuations of assets, particularly land.

Once house prices start to rise above their fundamental market values – for example, because interest rates have fallen and it is cheaper to take out a mortgage – speculation ensures that prices do not return to their fundamental values but, rather, continue to grow rapidly. Although owner-occupiers buy because they want to live in their own home – the motivation is use, not investment or speculation – homeowners in the UK are aware that buying is, across most stages of the economic cycle, a better investment than renting.

We all recognise the times when memories of negative equity are forgotten, and the talk is of 'trading up' to a house of greater investment value and of 'getting on the housing ladder' before a starter home becomes permanently unaffordable. These are signs that there is more than a slight speculative tinge to the property market, that house buyers are significantly influenced by the prospect of capital gains.

At some point this spiral comes to an end, as people are unwilling to borrow the sums needed to sustain it. This may happen for any number of reasons including an economic slowdown, higher costs of borrowing, political uncertainty or rumours that house prices are going to fall. It usually coincides with the time that new buildings (most recently two-bedroom flats and office space) come on to the market after the inevitable lag between the decision to build and completion of the buildings.

Prices level off. If there are factors making it difficult for people to make the payments on their mortgages, such as high interest rates or unemployment, they may be forced to sell; homes are repossessed, and prices fall. Recent buyers may be left with negative equity and are unable to move home – for example, to find a new job. Banks that have lent against the security of over-valued properties face losses – and possibly even failure – if their borrowers are unable to keep up with interest payments.

As we saw so dramatically in 2008, the damage caused is to the whole system as well as to individuals. Failures of banks and other financial institutions damage confidence, require enormous bailouts by the taxpayer and make credit more expensive and more difficult to obtain. Consumers and businesses cut back spending and overall levels of demand fall. The result is a reduction in economic growth, recession and even depression.

One reason that housing investment is so important in the functioning of the economy is that so many people are unavoidably drawn into it. No one needs to invest in tulips, or railways, but everyone needs a home. Even at what is obviously the peak of the housing market people need to move home, and either take the risk that prices will fall or choose the uncertainties and disadvantages of renting. While most homeowners are not speculators, they are drawn into a speculative market; one in which it might be difficult to believe that house prices will ever again fall.

Another reason house prices are so important for the economy is that most homeowners are only able to buy a house by borrowing a large proportion of the cost from a bank or building society. This leverage leaves the borrower vulnerable to even quite small falls in property values as well as to rising interest rates.

Buy-to-let and commercial landlords are, for much of the economic cycle, investors rather than speculators with rental income greater than their costs. But, in the few years before a housing bubble bursts, speculation begins to dominate the market and landlords contribute to stoking up the bubble by buying more property. This has been exacerbated by the UK tax system, which, in 2006, provided over £2 billion in tax relief on interest payments to buy-to-let landlords (Guardian money 23/6/07:6), encouraging them to borrow the highest possible proportion of the purchase price. In the 2008 housing crash it became clear that some properties had been deliberately overvalued to maximise this tax relief.

Bubbles and economic growth

The most obvious direction for the link between asset prices and economic growth is that fluctuation in the level of economic activity causes fluctuation in asset prices. But a close look at the timing of events at the end of a period of explosive growth suggests that asset prices lead, and so may drive, economic activity. A peak in the rate of return on property is a good predictor of a downturn in the economy a year later (RICS 1994:30).

The collapse of a bubble in the stock or housing market is known to lead to slowing of economic growth, and sometimes to recession. The bursting of a house price (that is, land price) bubble is more likely to have an impact on the banking system, and the whole economy, than the bursting of a stock market bubble. Bordo and Jeanne (2002) surveyed the experience in Organisation of Economic Co-operation and Development (OECD) countries since 1970 and found that, out of 24 booms in equities, only three (one in eight) were followed by busts, while the 19 booms in property prices were followed by 10 busts (more than one in two)(International Monetary Fund 2003:61).

There have been some notable examples. In the early 1980s the Savings and Loan crisis in the U.S., caused by imprudent real estate lending in a deregulated market, required a government bailout of over $120 billion and was a major cause of the subsequent recession. In the 1990s, the Japanese banking crisis was also caused by a failure of regulation and the expansion of credit as banks lent against overvalued property assets. The economic damage amounted to over 10 per cent of Japanese GDP and led to over a decade of deflation and economic stagnation.

The efficient market hypothesis holds that asset price bubbles are impossible when markets are efficient. But Herring and Wachter (1999) have identified inefficiencies in the housing market – speculation, disaster myopia, perverse incentives and banking employees incentivised to make risky loans while the banks themselves know that the taxpayer will bail them out.

The consequences of the 2007 house price collapse in the U.S., followed by the banking crisis and global recession, should have made us sufficiently aware of the damage done by speculative land price bubbles to feel the need to do something to prevent them.

While quasi-cyclical fluctuations in activity are to be expected in a complex dynamic system like the economy, house price bubbles have more destructive consequences than other precipitating factors because such a large proportion of the population is involved in buying a home, and because we do so with borrowed money.

Smoothing out economic growth

Keynes suggested that involuntary unemployment and under-utilisation of economic capacity were due to insufficient demand in the economy and proposed that the state should manage the level of aggregate demand throughout the economic cycle (John Maynard Keynes). He proposed that, at times of economic downturn, the government should spend more than it received in taxes, deficit financing, thereby creating new demand. This would be balanced by increases in taxation during the boom phase.

It is now widely believed that, in the medium to long term, this sort of deficit financing fails to stimulate demand and fuels inflation in both consumer prices and asset prices. As money is introduced into the economy, some is used for current consumption while some is saved and invested. Investment in land is not available for investment in production and does not give rise to any increase in economic activity. The new money leads to rising land prices and becomes locked up in these land values. If the new money could be prevented from finding its way into land values, deficit financing would produce a more sustained boost to demand. We need to make sure that money introduced to stimulate the economy does something more useful than boosting house prices.

Interest rates

Interest rates are a key mechanism by which central banks control the money supply by influencing the demand for credit. The government is able to set the interest rate on safe investments (government bonds) and this provides a floor below which interest rates for other investments will not fall – if this level of return is available from the government, why lend on more risky investments unless you will earn more in interest?

Long-term interest rates are determined in the market by the supply and demand for credit. A borrower will have to pay at least as much as the lender could obtain from another borrower with the same risk of default. The government is usually the borrower least likely to default on their loan, so the long-term interest rate for low-risk lending is determined in the market for government bonds.

In an ownership economy, central banks set the short-term interest rate at which they lend to financial institutions, and they conduct open market operations in which buying bonds increases the supply of money available to banks and so reduces interest rates.

A rational economic agent will give attention not to the nominal rate of interest (the payment that you actually make for a loan) but to the real rate of interest (the nominal rate of interest minus inflation). The real rate of interest is influenced by the riskiness of the loan, the supply and demand for credit and government policy.

Monetary policy and inflation

The rate of consumer price inflation is the annual percentage increase in the price of a representative basket of goods and services purchased by consumers. The current basket used in the UK is the Consumer Prices Index (CPI), which includes no element that is directly related to house prices.

The stated purpose of monetary policy is to ensure stable prices and confidence in the currency, while providing the conditions for non-inflationary growth. Absolute price stability, zero per cent inflation, may not be achievable or even desirable in an ownership economy. Inflation avoids the risks of deflation and 'oils' the economy where money is issued as debt, providing a continuing stimulus to growth as well as allowing wages to fall in real terms without a nominal wage cut and the humiliation of that group of workers that this would signal.

74

The principal mechanism for influencing the money supply is the Bank of England interest rate, the base rate. Increasing interest rates reduces consumer price inflation after a long and not entirely predictable delay.

Because the measure of inflation, the Consumer Prices Index (CPI), is chosen to exclude housing costs, the control of inflation is not intended to control inflation of asset prices. This is the result of deliberate choices by the Treasury, which stripped mortgage interest payments out of the Retail Price Index (RPI) after the UK's ejection from the European Exchange Rate Mechanism in 1992 and removed all housing costs in 2003 when it adopted the CPI in place of the RPI. Even when consumer price inflation is held down, for example to targets of 2–3 per cent, the prices of assets like land and shares may increase much more rapidly – as we saw in 2006–7.

During the boom years there was disagreement amongst academics and central bankers about whether monetary policy should target asset price inflation at all, even though the role of asset price inflation in creating economic slowdowns was well understood.

It might seem incongruous that the clamour of advice to central banks to cut interest rates when asset prices fall is not matched by calls to raise interest rates when asset prices rise. But such a course of action, aimed at holding down the price of homes and shares, would be deeply unpopular. So central banks either fail to restrain asset prices or actually encourage them in the knowledge that they cause a short-term boom.

It may anyway not be possible for central banks to make much difference – asset price inflation is only weakly responsive to changes in interest rates. When house prices are rising at 20 per cent per year they will not be halted, even if interest rates are raised to 10 per cent, a rate that would do real damage to business.

Stewardship economy

Boom and bust

As previously explained, one of the greatest advantages of a stewardship economy, compared with an ownership economy, is that speculation in land prices is not possible as land has no market value. This means that house price bubbles – with their attendant damage to economic growth, the banking sector and individual wealth – cannot happen.

A stewardship economy automatically provides a higher level of aggregate demand than an ownership economy, by distributing the market rent of land. Stewardship fees are recycled as Universal Income and this increases the income of everyone, including poorer people who are the most likely to spend it on current consumption. Land prices do not rise, and new money is not locked up in the private gains of landowners. This increased demand is maximal during the boom phase and tends to reinforce the economic cycle rather than counteract it. So, there may continue to be some need for counter-cyclical intervention to reduce demand during booms and support it during busts, as in ownership economies.

As people do not invest in land in a stewardship economy, monetary or fiscal policy designed to introduce demand into the economy has the desired effect of stimulating economic activity rather than the undesirable one of funding house price inflation.

Interest rates

In a stewardship economy the rate of interest is the market price of credit and depends on the supply and demand for credit. There are important differences from an ownership economy in both the supply and demand for credit.

The central bank that has introduced full reserve banking is able to tackle inflation (or recession) by directly withdrawing money from (or injecting money into) the economy. It would not need to raise (or lower) interest rates for this purpose, and they could be left to be determined in the market.

In a stewardship economy there is no need for long-term government borrowing as it receives from the Land Stewardship Trust the revenue that it requires both for current spending and for investment.

The level of business borrowing in a stewardship economy is difficult to predict. Borrowing to purchase land is unnecessary but greater economic activity leads to increased business borrowing. Household borrowing is likely to be lower in a stewardship economy as the amount of each mortgage is less than in ownership economies because it needs to cover only the value of the buildings, not the land as well.

It is difficult to predict whether there will be an increase in household renting as the financial incentives to own your home are removed, or a reduction in renting as the role of landlord becomes less attractive. This means that the total number of mortgages, like other areas of household borrowing, is uncertain.

Overall, the total demand for borrowing in a stewardship economy should be less than in an ownership economy operating at the same level of output. Lower levels of demand for credit lead to lower interest rates.

When interest rates are low, as they may be in a stewardship economy, there is a greater incentive to borrow the cheap money and to invest in assets. Share price bubbles are likely to be more intense in these conditions. Although bubbles in land prices don't occur in a stewardship economy, bubbles in share prices will need careful attention.

Real interest rates also influence the importance we give to the future. If interest rates are indeed low in a stewardship economy this will make it easier for us to take a much more long-term view of future generations and the future of the planet.

Monetary policy and inflation

As land has no market value in a stewardship economy, central banks are able to target consumer price inflation and foster economic growth without needing to consider land prices or house price bubbles. They might, however, be wise to include housing costs in the CPI.

It is sometimes suggested that a proprietor (owner or steward of land) might pass taxes and charges on the market rent of land on to a tenant or customer and thereby fuel inflation. They might try to pass it on to a tenant. But if the tenant was able to pay a higher rent, why had the landlord not increased the rent before the tax or charge was introduced? The landlord risks losing her tenant. The owner occupier of a business site might try to pass the charge or tax on to the customer through higher prices. But in an ownership economy, competition from less desirable sites keeps consumer prices down, and the higher level of rent is not passed on. The same applies to stewardship fees, which are no more than rents paid to the collective rather than to a private landlord.

Environmental fees and charges are different from stewardship fees in that they do contribute to consumer price inflation. The reason is that they are applied uniformly to the whole economy – the carbon cost of petrol is the same wherever the petrol station is located. Environmental fees and charges are doing what they are intended to do – to reduce demand for environmentally damaging products by raising their price. It is important to allow this to happen.

Consumers can be reassured that these price increases are counterbalanced by the Environmental Dividend that is paid to everyone. They will benefit if they consume less than average amounts of goods and services that damage the environment and be out of pocket only if they consume more than their fair share. It is essential that the government stands firm in the face of protests against the rising cost of fuel, for example.

Trades Unions will want to ensure that their members' living standards are not eroded by environmental charges. But if they ignore the new income that everyone receives as their Environmental Dividend and press for increased wages in response to inflation, they will instigate a wage-price spiral that generates ongoing and increasing inflation.

In a stewardship economy there is a risk that the Bank of England might increase interest rates in response to the price increases caused by environmental fees in an attempt to head off a wage-price spiral. This would miss the point of the price increases and the tightening of monetary policy would risk slowing growth and even recession.

In summary: As is appropriate in the management of a complex dynamic system, stewardship offers a way to stabilise the economy by rethinking the fundamental institutional arrangements. Stewardship removes the speculative element that fuels property price bubbles and their subsequent collapse. Economic cycles will still be a feature of stewardship economies with irrational exuberance in shares, commodities and financial instruments. But land and housing, and so those of us who are engaged in using resources rather than speculating, will cease to play a part. And when the government needs to counteract the cycle of boom and bust its fiscal and monetary measures will have the desired effect on demand rather than their effects being dissipated in the housing market.

Stewardship fees cannot be passed on to the consumer through price increases, and so are not inflationary.Stewardship permits a more direct control of inflation than is possible in an ownership economy, and interest rates are likely to be lower. While low interest rates make it easier for us to give proper consideration to the future of our children and grandchildren, it will also require us to ensure that savings are available for investment.

Part II   Global economy

Chapter 6 International stewardship

This chapter explores the possibilities that arise when two or more states adopt stewardship and use this shared background to grow economic co-operation. It first identifies some of the problems associated with international issues such as free trade, international investment and aid. It then introduces the idea of 'International Stewardship', the practice of sharing stewardship fees across more than one state and suggests how this practice would ensure that everyone benefits from free trade. It then extends this principle to sharing the rents of natural resources like oil and water as an International Environmental Dividend;   and describes the implications of these measures for peace building and for migration.

Ownership economy

Free trade

Debates about the costs and benefits of globalisation have raged for the last two hundred years. The Corn Laws of the 19th century protected British agriculture and agricultural jobs, but at the expense of high food prices and great suffering on the general population. The laws were introduced in 1815 as Britain began to open its markets after the Napoleonic wars and were eventually repealed in 1846. The great globalisation of the 19th century had begun. Reaction against free trade followed in the 1870s, with Europe protecting its agriculture from grain imports and America protecting its manufacturing industries.

Protectionism has persisted through the 20th and into the 21st century in spite of the development of free trade areas like the European Union. It is growing in response to the current recession, as demonstrated by public opposition to the Canadian Economic Trading Area (CETA) and Transatlantic Trade and Investment Partnership (TTIP) agreements and providing the backdrop to both the British Brexit referendum and Donald Trump's election in 2016.

Some geographical specialisation in production is understandable and appropriate – agriculture in fertile areas, heavy engineering in areas of coal and iron ore deposits, for example. Some is the legacy of historical accident; once a region becomes a centre for a particular activity there are advantages for other similar or linked businesses to cluster in that area.

Adam Smith advocated free trade on the grounds that trading partners are each able to produce some goods more cheaply than the other (1776 Volume II Book IV Chapter II:260) – that each has an absolute advantage in the production of at least one sort of good. David Ricardo (1817) extended this argument to show that trade is beneficial to both parties even when each has only a comparative advantage in some products. Here each sells things that they can produce with relative (comparative) efficiency and buys other products that they can produce only with relative inefficiency.

Consumers in both parties (countries) should benefit from lower prices of products, and both economies should flourish, as each is producing the goods most suited to their circumstances. Free Trade should then ensure that production takes place at the lowest possible cost. Foreign competition may be expected to stimulate domestic companies to become more productive, and technology imports provide the means for them to do so. The increase in efficiency benefits the consumer and the global economy as a whole: that is the theory.

David Ricardo's key assumption underlying free trade was that importing an item would free up production capacity at home, which would be used to produce something else (1817). He assumed that there would be full employment (of labour and capital) and that neither labour nor capital are internationally mobile.

Paul Ekins (1993:3) identifies a number of other assumptions on which the theory of comparative advantage rests. It assumes that neither partner will externalise costs, for example by damaging the environment or society; that a country developing an advantage in technology will not use this to develop an even greater technological advantage over the course of time; that there are no imbalances of power that cause the terms of trade to be coercive;

and that specialisation does not leave either trading partner vulnerable in a rapidly changing world.

These assumptions are unrealistic, however, and people participate in trade not just as consumers but as workers and savers. Some individuals are harmed by trade even when their country benefits overall.

Adam Smith and David Ricardo did not foresee the way in which unemployment would be a persistent feature of ownership economies. 'Freeing up' labour often results not in its redeployment to more productive activities but in increasing unemployment. Imports of products may be mirrored by the export of jobs, as investors transfer capital abroad rather than investing in new ventures at home. Jobs are created in some industries and some countries and lost in others.

Where labour is internationally mobile a country may lose skilled workers who can see better prospects for satisfactory employment abroad, and this 'brain drain' provokes a further downward spiral in economic activity. Where the scale of migration is large, population changes may impose strains on the recipient country as well as the country of origin.

Countries with high production costs and a lack of unique products decline with a shrinking economy, rising unemployment and falling investment. They pay a high cost for the short-term advantage of cheap imports. Countries with low production costs, unique products or low environmental and social standards prosper and develop a growing economy, lower unemployment, stronger currencies and greater levels of investment. This comes at the cost of subsidising consumers in countries with high production costs. And rising costs of production (the costs of labour, land and the support of an ageing population) sow the seeds of the eventual decline of their economy.

High-consumption economies want access to supplies of commodities (especially agricultural and forest products, minerals and oil) that are produced by low-consumption economies. These low-consumption economies want access to the manufactured goods that the high-consumption economies produce. The 1970s and 1980s saw inexorably rising prices for manufactured goods while commodity prices, although fluctuating at times wildly, did not rise in parallel. The terms of trade for low-consumption economies deteriorated, and their economies suffered as a result.

The volatility of commodity prices is destructive in its own right. The fate of producers in low-consumption economies, who may have to decide what crops to plant a season or two ahead of the harvest, is in the hands of commodity traders in high-consumption economies who establish the world prices. A variety of solutions to this problem have been proposed, such as the holding of buffer stocks to provide a cushion for prices or financial methods for stabilising export earnings. The most hopeful has been the growth of the Fair Trade movement, which exploits the 1000 per cent difference between retail prices in high-consumption economies and the price paid to producers. Fair trade dealers can afford to pay a few pence extra to the producer which may double his or her income and at the same time place regular orders that allow producers to plan ahead, while imposing only a small premium on the sale price.

The prices of many products seem too good to be true, and they are. We may protest when we hear about documented cases of child and slave labour, hazardous working conditions and the denial of the right to join a union but we must suspect that these practices are widespread, not the exception. In a similar way we should not be surprised when we hear about the discharge of toxic waste and pollution in low-consumption economies that are struggling to establish their advantage in the global trading system. We even find it morally acceptable to transport waste of various sorts to low-consumption economies for processing.

A weak economy may try to insulate itself from decline by adopting protectionist measures to prevent free trade – it may erect tariff or non-tariff barriers to imports, or it may subsidise exports. These measures protect local jobs and enterprise in the short run, but removal of foreign competition isolates domestic firms from the need to develop and innovate. The costs, to government paying for export subsidies and to consumers paying unnecessarily high prices for products, may be high. Other countries retaliate by adopting similar measures, thus increasing costs and reducing world trade which itself threatens jobs and enterprises.

The Organisation for Economic Co-operation and Development (OECD) has estimated that losses due to tariff and non-tariff barriers deny an income to low-consumption economies that is twice as great as the amounts they receive as aid.

Many high-consumption economies subsidise, in one way or another, exports to low-consumption economies. This is most problematic with agricultural subsidies, where dumping of produce lowers the price of food and undermines the capacity of local farmers. It is also a problem with manufactured goods, where it is local manufacturing that is undermined. The subsidised export of armaments is particularly destructive.

Wherever there is free movement of goods and capital, economic activity flourishes in some areas more than in others. Even if free trade is beneficial to consumers and to the global economy, some areas bear the costs while others reap the benefits. Trade offers one of the most powerful opportunities for the development of low-consumption economies, but the experience has often been problematic and sometimes downright exploitative.

Financial support for areas that lose from free trade is not a sop to political pressure but an essential element that is required to make free trade fair and therefore acceptable. Paul Samuelson showed that, even where one country loses and another wins from free trade, both countries would choose free trade in their own self-interest if the winner were to compensate the loser with an 'ideal lump-sum reallocation' (Samuelson, 1962).

Transfers to low-consumption economies

Remittances

Low-consumption economies receive a greater income in the form of workers' remittances than the amount they receive in aid (Dilip Ratha 2003).

Investment

An increasingly important aspect of the relationship between high-consumption economies and low-consumption economies is commercial investment – both loans by banks and direct investment by institutional and individual investors. In the 1970s investment was driven by the banks, seeking outlets for the large petroleum revenues deposited by the oil states after the dramatic oil price rises agreed by OPEC in 1973; in the 1980s it was driven by investors seeking higher returns on their capital than could be obtained in high-consumption countries with their relatively low interest rates. Banks discovered that their loans were more risky than they had anticipated as debtors defaulted, and since the 1990s flows of capital have proved fickle even though they have remained significant.

Aid

Some aid is given to low-consumption economies for humanitarian purposes. This may be to combat emergency situations like drought or earthquake, or to support longer-term development, such as agricultural support. This sort of aid may come from individual charitable donations or government funds, and it is often channelled through non-governmental organisations or multilateral agencies like the World Bank.

Bilateral aid, by contrast, is linked to the interests of the donor country. This may be political, for example to improve political relationships or to exert pressure on the recipient around human rights or environmental issues. Or it may be economic, for example where the aid is tied to purchases from the donor, which may include arms and other manufactured goods or to services such as consultants from the donor country.

Aid in the form of a loan may threaten the recipient with long-lasting indebtedness and dependence. The legacy of such 'aid' has in many cases been inappropriate infrastructure and the undermining of local economies through the dumping of goods.

But a World Bank review (David Dollar & Lant Pritchett 1998) concluded that aid at the level of 1 per cent of the recipient's current GDP leads to a sustained increase in the country's rate of growth of 0.5 per cent in countries with good governance and good economic policies. Good in this context means the rule of law, competent bureaucracy, low inflation and openness to trade. And this growth reduces poverty. In countries where governance and economic management are bad, however, aid actually reduces growth a little.

The lessons from the past are that large infrastructure projects like dams bring the least benefit. Measures to develop both transport and internet links in countries that are poorly connected to international trade and business may be helpful.

The Copenhagen Consensus Project (Evans 2003) attempted to develop international consensus about the most cost-effective issues for intervention in low-consumption economies. The top priorities that it identified were infectious diseases, particularly HIV, malaria and TB; malnutrition; trade liberalisation through the removal of tariffs and subsidies; water; and sanitation.

Exchange rates and single currency areas

Unequal development

Trade causes particular problems where a country's currency is shared by its trading partner so it can't compete by allowing its exchange rate to fall. This is the reason why both individual countries and free trade zones put in place transfer programmes within their boundaries which support areas that suffer poor employment and growth. The European Union has had a series of programmes like Objective 1 that provide aid to areas to foster their 'regeneration'. But these programmes have been time-limited which limits the impact they are able to have.

Inappropriate interest rates

One of the few ways in which an ownership economy can adjust its money supply is by setting appropriate interest rates. In a large and diverse currency union, such as the Euro area, interest rates are always likely to be too high in areas that are in recession and too low in areas where the economy is booming.

Population movements

People move between countries, just as they move within a country, for a wide variety of reasons. Apart from short-term visits for business and pleasure, people may relocate to live with family and friends or to benefit from higher education or training. They may flee wars or have a well-founded fear of persecution and seek asylum as a refugee. But the main reason that people move is to seek work to raise their living standards. This is a powerful motivation in ownership economies – just as capital migrates to areas of prosperity, so do people in search of work. This may benefit the global economy, some countries and the mobile individuals. High-consumption economies generally find that immigrants are younger and bring hard work, enterprise and thrift to fill jobs that local people do not want.

Inequalities between ownership economies set up a powerful incentive for people to migrate for economic reasons. And high-consumption economies additionally stimulate economic migration through the activity of their hidden economies – employers who wish to evade tax employ migrants who do not have the right to work and are trapped in low pay, poor conditions and secrecy.

Economic migration causes problems. It may reinforce international differences in prosperity and wealth, particularly when the people leaving a low-consumption economy are the most highly qualified and skilled; there are more Ghanaian doctors in New York than in the whole of Ghana. This sets up cultural and economic tensions, particularly in times of recession. At the same time, remittances from these migrants to their country of origin are an important source of income for their families.

The International Office for Migration would like to see people make decisions about emigration from choice not necessity. This will only happen if low-consumption economies become prosperous and provide jobs for local people.

Environment

Environmental charges

In an ownership economy when one group of countries introduces environmental charges or taxes their prices increase, and their producers find themselves at a competitive disadvantage compared with producers from other countries. Understandably, producers and workers either lobby against environmental measures or seek to impose tariffs on products imported from countries that do not impose environmental charges, to 'level the playing field'.

Water

Wars have been fought over water resources at least since 2nd century BCE when a war in the Aosta valley in Italy was caused by a dispute over access to water. Conflicts persist to the present day – in 1967 rivalry over water rights was an important factor in the conflict that culminated in the Six Day War.

Fred Pearce (2006:203) points out that the Nile, Danube, Rhine, Niger, Congo and Zambezi each pass through at least eight countries. Almost half the world's population live in international river basins and two thirds of these have no treaties for sharing their water. Even where treaties exist, these are the result of historical processes and the exercise of power, not a commitment to handle current realities fairly. The ownership of water rights has evolved in the same sort of haphazard and coercive way as the ownership of land.

The most serious opportunities for conflict centre on water abstraction by upstream nations, particularly by dam building. Many downstream countries are highly vulnerable – more than twenty nations get more than half their water from their neighbours. Egypt is currently dependent on treaty rights for its claim to the bulk of the flow of the Nile; Pakistan is dependent on the Indus and is vulnerable to damming of its tributaries by India; Jordan lost most of its supply from the River Jordan in 1964 when Israel diverted water from the Sea of Galilee to its National Water Carrier; and Syria and Iraq are dependent on the Tigris and Euphrates which are both currently being dammed in Turkey. And conflicts about water will become more severe as climate change advances.

Stewardship economy

This section considers the impact of a stewardship economy on the global economy.

Free trade

Comparative advantage

Suppose that stewardship is introduced into just one country. A firm in that country which rents its premises faces land charges that are unchanged. It continues to pay rent and is not concerned about the payment of stewardship fees by its landlord. All or some of the burden of taxes that it faces, including those on labour, are removed so it becomes more profitable than an otherwise similar firm in a country that has not introduced stewardship. For this sort of firm, the introduction of stewardship provides it with a comparative advantage. As has been pointed out previously, this advantage does not extend to a firm that owns the land on which it operates, whose gains from the removal of taxes are very broadly balanced by the requirement to pay stewardship fees. A firm that acts as a landlord is less profitable in a stewardship economy, and therefore suffers a comparative disadvantage. However, it is unusual for landlords in one country to be in a competitive market with landlords in another country.

On the whole, a stewardship economy adopted by a lone country will increase the country's comparative advantage.

Transfers to low-consumption economies

In an established global stewardship economy, remittances from high to low consumption economies will probably be lower than they are now, as fewer people have to move abroad to find work. Investment is not discouraged by taxation on income and capital gains so there should be more investment in low consumption economies than now.

Voluntary transfers of aid are likely to continue to take place, but the most intriguing possibilities arise when stewardship fees are shared across international borders – International Stewardship. This is, of course, not 'aid' but a recognition of the right of everyone to an equal share of the wealth of the natural world.

International Stewardship

At the scale of the state, stewardship redistributes (or predistributes, as James Robertson would say) wealth from those who use more than their equal share of the land and environment to those who use less. The underlying ethical principle, that everyone has the right to an equal share of the wealth of the natural world, suggests that this distribution should take place on a global scale. The scale that is politically possible will depend ultimately on the scale of society to which people recognise themselves as belonging, and across which they are therefore prepared to allow distribution to occur.

Sharing stewardship fees across national boundaries

A stewardship economy that shares fees across national boundaries provides a mechanism by which automatic transfer payments are made from areas of high per capita land value to areas of low per capita land value, and so from high-consumption economies to low-consumption economies. This 'International Stewardship' requires no cumbersome bureaucratic process to administer and evaluate and is not time limited. It just naturally provides the sort of cross-subsidisation of poor areas by rich areas that is needed to counteract the unequal development that otherwise already exists and may be exacerbated by free trade. It is achieved if: two or more states pool the stewardship fees they receive; some of this pool of revenue is used to fund investment for shared or global objectives; the rest of the pool of revenue is paid to the participating states, either to distribute on an equal per capita basis as Universal Income to the whole population of the states or to fund development.

- The revenue from stewardship fees would provide a powerful stimulus to demand in local economies, whether it was used for infrastructure investment or as a Universal Income.

Necessary conditions for free trade that is fair

International Stewardship provides people with real financial benefits when economic growth occurs in other countries. It compensates the poor, both individuals and countries, for losses that they incur from free trade which makes free trade both more fair and more acceptable politically. It supports the long-term viability of the international economic order, as well as supporting social justice, by providing a regular payment equivalent to the 'ideal lump-sum reallocation'.

International Stewardship makes it possible for participant states to engage in free trade and to remove protectionist trade barriers and subsidies.

International Environmental Dividend

Just as International Stewardship would pool stewardship fees and distribute an International Universal Income, so it would be possible to pool revenue from environmental permits and distribute an International Environmental Dividend. This would be appropriate where the countries involved have the same environmental standards, for example if they were all equal participants in the European Emissions Trading Scheme. However, if one country adopts higher environmental standards than another, and so experiences higher (true cost) prices, it should distribute its Environmental Dividend nationally not internationally.

Transnational and global interventions

A small number of critically important things truly require global oversight. These include climate change, infectious diseases, security, the financial system and the internet.

One of the reasons why the United Nations, and global bodies like the World Health Organisation, have proved to be so ineffective is that they have been denied significant secure funding. If several countries were to participate in International Stewardship, there would be a pool of revenue from shared stewardship fees that could be used to enable these bodies to achieve their goals.

Transition to International Stewardship

Transition to International Stewardship would be easiest when the relevant countries had introduced domestic stewardship at about the same time and were at similar levels of per capita consumption.

One way of approaching transition to International Stewardship would be to share amongst participating countries a progressively greater proportion of the pot of revenue from stewardship fees, starting, say, with 5 per cent of the pot in the first year and increasing by another 5 per cent each year until Universal Incomes (or similar per capita transfers) were equal after 20 years. This could involve an agreement between two countries, between all the countries in a free trade area, or even globally. It would be necessary to give attention to the withdrawal of subsidies, and to harmonisation of other taxes.

Exchange Rates and single currency areas

If a domestic economy grows, especially if it is accompanied by increased investment and inward migration, there is a risk that the currency will strengthen. This would harm the domestic manufacturing industry but would reduce the costs of imports.

It will be important to model the consequences for the exchange rate, and it is possible there might need to be some restrictions on inward investment and currency movements for countries that do not implement stewardship.

Population movements

Wealthy people would have a financial incentive to live in a country that is an early adopter of stewardship, either staying there or moving there, because they would then be free from taxes like Income Tax and Capital Gains Tax. The cost to them would be the stewardship fees of desirable homes and places to do business. Poor people would be attracted by the growing economy and the Universal Income. People on a middle income have less to gain, either from exemption from Income Tax or from Universal Income. The tax changes would, even so, make such a country an attractive place to live and the country would almost certainly need to strengthen its restrictions on immigration.

International Stewardship provides a Universal Income for all those who live in the participating states. In low consumption economies this influx of Universal Income stimulates local demand and economic opportunities. People then don't need to move location to gain a share of the wealth generated by the global economy. This is likely to make it possible to lower the barriers to migration in a stewardship world.

Movement of Investment

If a single country adopts a stewardship economy when others do not, banks in that country might wish to move investments elsewhere, believing they would be more secure in jurisdictions where land values could be used as collateral. On the other hand, if the national economy were strong, as would be expected in a stewardship economy freed from the deadweight loss of taxation, this strength would be likely to counteract any tendency to shift investment abroad.

Environment

International Stewardship Trusts

Water

Disputes about water are only likely to become more insistent as dependence on water resources becomes more pressing with climate change. Stewardship offers an approach to water rights that states could choose to put in place. They would be most likely to do so if they have already put in place stewardship of water within their own borders.

An international approach to the stewardship of water, just like a national approach, is implemented at the scale of a watershed. This requires states to set up a joint Watershed Stewardship Trust, for each river basin, which has the responsibility of managing its water resources sustainably and of ensuring that everyone gets fair (equal) access to the benefits of this water.

Equal access to water would mean that the water available for abstraction should be allocated between the countries in proportion to their populations. This approach would be fair but also inefficient because it does not take account of the different uses to which water may be put in each country. For example, if one country is fertile and one is barren, the most efficient use of water might be to allocate more to the country that can make best use of it.

Allocation would be efficient as well as fair if any country that abstracts surface or ground water has to surrender abstraction permits that it buys from the Watershed Stewardship Trust. The Trust then distributes this revenue to the countries in proportion to the size of their populations living in the watershed. In this way countries that abstract more than their equal share compensate countries that abstract less than their equal share.

This proposal relates to a steady-state stewardship world. As with land ownership, current treaty allocations may be far from these equal per capita benefits. Transition would be complex and would need to be gradual and carefully designed.

International commons

There are at present areas of the natural world that are not the sole property of a single state. These may be held in trust for all of humankind (like sea-bed mineral resources), administered by international treaty (like Antarctica), managed as an open access regime (the oceans) or managed as a common property regime (fisheries, satellite orbits).

In a world of stewardship economy each of these are held in Trust. An international Stewardship Trust manages the resource and receives income from stewardship fees or permits paid by those who use it. Simply establishing clear title and private property rights is itself a significant intervention, while a functioning Stewardship Trust would share the wealth derived from the resource amongst the whole population.

Environmental charges

In a stewardship economy, the introduction of a new environmental charge reduces the profits of producers, and this in turn reduces the stewardship fees that they are able to offer for the land they use. Their overall costs are unchanged, and they are not put at a disadvantage to international competitors. There is therefore no need to impose tariffs on products imported from countries that do not impose environmental charges to 'level the playing field,' although such tariffs could be used to change the behaviour of foreign businesses that are not subject to environmental charges at home.

Conflict and peace-building

Conflict between states may be less likely if each is in itself a fair society in which all prosper, and no one has the need to identify an external enemy to blame for their condition.

The most frequent causes of conflict are disputes about territory and about natural resources – particularly water and oil – even though leaders may seek popular support on the grounds of national or religious difference. Such conflicts have, of course, been frequent in the past and present because the basis of claims to territory and resources has been widely assumed to be historical, and historical claims are almost inevitably overlapping and conflicted. Stewardship economies allocate land and resources, internally by asking the current claimant to compensate fairly all those who are excluded from their property, not on the basis of historical claims. Economies that accept this approach to allocation of land may seek solutions to international disputes by devising fair agreements rooted in present compensation rather than by resorting to historical claims. And if a dispute does arise, stewardship can suggest a mechanism for its resolution (see below).

Stewardship may contribute to peace-building and conflict resolution in a number of ways. It provides fair access to natural resources, promotes fair economic relationships and provides a framework for resolving territorial disputes.

Fair economic relationships

When one group is oppressed, or feels itself to be oppressed, by another group, the grievances may be expressed violently. Both within and between states, sharing the Universal Income and Environmental Dividend results in a reduction in economic oppression. The international transfer of stewardship fees is a visible manifestation of the interdependence between countries and ensures that people can see that trade is genuinely beneficial to each country.

The threat of excluding a country from International Stewardship would provide a powerful sanction against countries that act violently against their own populations or internationally.

Territorial disputes

The United Nations does not recognise the seizure of territory by force, though this has not put an end to the practice. If one country seizes part of another country it will incur costs, in lives and military expenditure but the victor will also benefit by the value of the land and natural resources that it has acquired. In a world in which International Stewardship is in place, the invader would find that it was taking on the obligation to share the market rent of its new territory with people in other countries. In this way, the economic incentive to claim and seize territory is less powerful in a stewardship world (Julian Pratt 2017 b: 9).

If this does not prove to be a sufficient deterrent to territorial disputes there may be another, non-military, approach to resolution. This auction-based approach, 'resolution by rent', draws on the same insights as stewardship but is entirely separate from it (Julian Pratt 2017 b: 12).

In summary: International Stewardship Economy

A group of countries can extend the principle of stewardship to their relationships with each other. They can decide to pool their stewardship fees to provide funding for transnational interventions and share the rest in proportion to the population size. International Stewardship provides an ongoing transfer of wealth from high-consumption economies to low-consumption economies. The revenue from stewardship fees could be distributed as a Universal

Income or used by governments to provide public goods, ideally at local level.

International Stewardship provides ways to manage natural resources, promote peace and help prevent territorial disputes. It ensures that all countries benefit from free trade and reduces the need for international. It does not require low-consumption economies to lower tariff barriers until they are ready to do so.

Environmental charges do not put domestic producers at a disadvantage compared with their international competitors. International Stewardship provides a way to manage the environment by pooling revenue from the auction of permits and sharing the resulting Environmental Dividend on an equal per capita basis.

Chapter 7   Low-consumption economies

This chapter brings us back to the most fundamental social issue of our time – poverty and suffering in low-consumption economies. Whether or not the International Stewardship described in the previous chapter is put into effect, stewardship is beneficial when put in place in low-consumption economies. It provides secure title to land, allocates land efficiently, redistributes wealth to the landless and ensures that everyone benefits from the wealth of natural resources like oil.

Ownership economy

Poverty and inequalities

One in four people living in low-consumption economies, about 1.4 billion people, live in extreme poverty (defined as a daily income of less than $1.25 in 2005) http://web.worldbank.org/poverty.

The most striking feature of the global economy is the way in which the last 250 years have brought unimaginable increases in wealth to some countries while others, particularly in sub-Saharan Africa, have hardly gained at all. In 1870 the world's richest countries had an average per capita income nine times greater than the poorest countries. By 1990 it was 45 times greater.

Does the inequality really matter, though, or is it just the absolute poverty that is harmful? Elsewhere I have suggested that inequalities in income within a country cause a range of problems including ill-health and crime, and that this is probably because inequalities affect people's sense of their social rank. This sense of rank only develops amongst people who are able to compare themselves with each other. Half a century ago most people in low-consumption economies would not have had enough information about high-consumption economies to make comparisons but there is nowhere now beyond the reach of television, mobile phone and the internet. It would be facile to blame the rise of anti-western sentiment entirely on these inequalities, but unwise to ignore their effect altogether.

Inequalities amongst the global population

Although there is general agreement that economic inequalities between nations are large and increasing, there is disagreement about whether the global population is becoming more or less unequal. This matters in the debate about globalisation and free trade because free traders believe that their policies benefit most people and reduce inequalities overall while protectionists believe that globalisation is causing increased inequality and poverty.

If you want to look at inequalities amongst the global population there are two ways to do this. One is to weight the per capita GDPs by the population of the country, treating the increasing average per capita income in the large populations of India and China as outweighing the stagnating or decreasing per capita income in sub-Saharan Africa. The other is to attribute income levels to everyone in the world and calculate some measure of inequality (such as the GINI coefficient).

The results are contested and depend on technical factors including the choice of whether to make comparisons across currencies using exchange rates or purchasing power parity. But it is probable that inequalities amongst the global population are decreasing, largely because of the remarkable growth in many Asian economies.

Causes of poverty

It is easy, but wrong, to attribute poverty entirely to exploitation of the poor by the rich, though there are situations in which this plays a part. There is no single cause of poverty. Geographical factors play a part – landlocked countries are generally poorer and grow more slowly than coastal nations as transport by sea is cheaper and easier than by land. Tropical countries, at least those with a significant agricultural sector, do worse than temperate ones – in part due to the burden of human and animal disease (Jeffrey Sachs 1997:21).

The most important factors, though, are security and governance. Countries with longstanding disputes and civil wars, lack of internal security, lawlessness, repression and corruption are likely to experience poverty. And a range of indicators – including average per capita GDP, income of the poorest 10 per cent of the population, life expectancy, political rights and environmental performance – are all highly correlated with an index of 'economic freedom' in a country. This index brings together measures of the security of property rights, low inflation, freedom to trade internationally, regulation, and size of government (James Gwartney & Robert Lawson 2007:27).

Land rights

An Oxfam publication suggests that the absence of secure land tenure systems lies at the heart of hunger and poverty in low-consumption economies (Claire Whittemore 1981). This absence of secure tenure impairs access to housing and also destroys the stability required for businesses investment.

Housing

In low-consumption economies people rarely have secure title to their land, even their homes. Most of the land is held by the government or in some form of customary tenure – less than 10 per cent of Africa is held in formal ownership.

Many countries have restrictions on land ownership that are intended to protect the poor and prevent exploitation by large landowners. Perversely these restrictions often make things worse for everyone by driving land transactions into the hidden economy.

Billions of people around the world live in slums. These are not temporary settlements – in Rio de Janeiro they have existed for over 100 years. The proximate cause is that the price of a legally owned site, serviced by utilities, is far higher than an informally owned and unserviced plot. There have been examples, for example in Bogota, where serviced plots of land have been made available at competitive prices by providing services and capturing the gains in land value to repay the investment (Claudio Acioly 2007:7).

Secure land rights improve the wealth of the poor by providing legal security when land is sold, rented or inherited. Studies in the Philippines showed that reducing the costs of land transactions and providing documentary evidence of secure legal title increases the value of property by about one third.

Enterprise and investment

Secure title to land provides an incentive to invest not just in homes but in agricultural improvements like terraces or irrigation, and in businesses.

The Peruvian economist Hernando de Soto (2000:6) suggests that entrepreneurs in low-consumption economies pay a high price for operating in the hidden sector – they have no access to capital in the form of loans or by issuing shares, and the only form of insurance available to them is the payment of protection money.

The most important source of funds for new businesses in the U.S. is a mortgage secured on the collateral of the entrepreneur's house. While people in low-consumption economies do save, and own assets such as houses, the legal titles to these assets are not strong enough to allow people to borrow and to create capital. Hernando de Soto proposes integrating existing extra-legal property arrangements into a formal property system that is available to everyone (2000:170). This could be expected to fuel local economic development in several ways, including providing people with collateral that allows them to borrow capital.

Experience in Peru and Argentina (Economist 28/8/2006:66) suggests that granting secure title does lead owners to improve their homes, enable them to obtain more loans from government sources, and loans at generally lower rates. It does not, however, seem to provide the poor with greater access to credit from commercial banks.

Secure land rights also make it possible for people to use the land more flexibly, making possible joint ownership ventures or sale when someone moves to find a job or leasing for someone beginning to farm or starting a business.

Civil society

The benefits of securing land rights for the poor go well beyond the economy. Land tenure systems generally discriminate against women which damages the whole of society. People occupying land without secure title are subject to intimidation by authorities who may use the threat of eviction to suppress criticism of abuses of power. Indeed, land policies lie at the root of social conflict in a wide range of countries.

Foreign ownership of land

Rising food prices since 2007 have led corporations and governments to acquire the freehold or long leasehold of large tracts of agricultural land in low-consumption economies in order to ensure national food security and access to biofuels (Guardian 22/11/08:30). South Korea and China have each acquired over 2 million hectares while Saudi Arabia and the United Arab Emirates each have over 1 million. Their largest landholdings are in Indonesia, Madagascar, Philippines, Sudan, Pakistan and Laos. The head of the UN Food and Agriculture Organisation has warned of the danger of poor states producing food for the rich at the expense of their own hungry people.

There may be benefits to the countries that sell their land in the form of an inflow of capital for development but there are indications that much of this is diverted by corrupt officials. The challenge is to find a way for this investment to provide a benefit to the low-consumption economy that is widely distributed and permanent.

Natural resources

'Curse of oil'

It is a distressing paradox that resource-rich countries generally grow more slowly and have worse levels of mortality and educational achievement than those that are resource-poor (Jeffrey Sachs 1995). One reason is economic. The currency appreciates when investment flows to a resource-rich country – the so-called 'Dutch disease'. This makes imports cheaper and exports more expensive, both of which undermine local industry and reduce employment levels. The oil industry generally employs a lot of specialist foreign workers and few local unskilled workers, with oil wealth concentrated in the hands of a few. And a government that gets its revenue from the oil industry rather than from taxation can lose interest in the wellbeing and support of its citizens.

The struggle to control access to the resource rents of oil and minerals, through corruption or violence, offers the reward of great wealth. Many studies have shown how this destabilises states and causes conflict:

- Mary Kaldor (2007) concludes that oil wars are caused by participants seeking the rent from the oilfields – they are 'rentier wars'.

- The International Committee of the Red Cross (2000) suggests that although many wars may begin in ethnic or ideological conflict they are sustained by trade in drugs, oil, minerals, timber or other resources and can best be understood as battles for resources.

- Paul Collier (World Bank 2001) has studied a large number of conflicts and civil wars and found that poverty and inequalities play an insignificant role. Conflict is more likely is when there are primary exports that are easily taxable by rebels.

These internal conditions are exacerbated by high-consumption economies that back both corrupt leaders and insurgent potential leaders to ensure their own continued access to oil and other resources.

Access to oil has clearly been a significant factor in recent military adventures, particularly in Iraq. One of the issues that has caused persisting instability in that country has been that Kurdish, Shia and Sunni populations each want their own territorial heartland to include contested oil deposits and they can use the oil revenues from these oil fields to finance their military activity.

Stewardship economy

Land rights have been at the heart of the colonial project and have taken the form of denial of common property rights, direct ownership and conflict over natural resources. The greatest indictment of our ownership world is the persistence of absolute poverty.

Poverty and inequalities

There are several reasons why there is less poverty in a stewardship world. Stewardship economies fare better than ownership economies, whether they are high- or low-consumption, because they have more efficient allocation of land, no taxes on work and enterprise and greater incentives to invest in infrastructure. In economies that are rich in natural resources stewardship provides a mechanism for capturing resource rents for the benefit of all, and so for reducing violence and corruption (Fred Harrison 2008:59). International Stewardship makes low consumption economies more economically rewarding places to live; it makes the terms of trade fairer, promotes peace and directly relieves poverty.

Land rights

There is a great deal that governments can do to provide secure legal rights to land including land registers, improving the legal status of property rights, reducing the costs of land transactions and resolving boundary disputes. These are all steps that a country would necessarily take in preparation for embarking on a transition to stewardship.

A stewardship economy provides stewards with secure title to their land. This encourages them to invest in and improve their homes. Governments (local and national) can fund investment in water, drainage, electricity and transport infrastructure from the anticipated increases in stewardship fees, just as they can in high-consumption economies. In this way slums can be replaced by secure owner-occupation.

Stewardship provides businesses as well as homeowners with security of tenure, an incentive to invest in buildings and improvements and the conditions necessary for flexible land use. But there is a potential problem. The land itself has no market value and so the only asset that could be used as collateral for loans would be improvements on the land. The poor in a stewardship economy benefit from the Universal Income but their access to credit would only improve if lenders changed their behaviour to focus more on business plans and ability to pay than on ownership of collateral.

A stewardship economy provides secure land rights for the whole population as an essential aspect of the economy, not as an optional extra. This reduces the potential for conflict, eviction, intimidation and discrimination against women.

Stewardship ensures that the market rent of the land of a country is collected from all those acting as stewards and distributed to the whole population, and that this continues for ever. It prevents foreign owners from exporting the market rent of the land as they frequently do in an ownership economy (though they can still export profits earned by conducting business). For this reason, stewardship may be recognised as a particularly appropriate approach where there is a significant amount of land held by absentee landlords or by oligarchs who have a near-monopoly on land and natural resources.

Indigenous peoples

A stewardship economy acknowledges the history of indigenous peoples and recognise their rights to common or collective property rights to their traditional land and territories. The main advantage of stewardship for indigenous peoples is that there is less incentive for anyone to try to profit from the extraction of natural resources and the exploitation of their land. No individual or corporation can profit from resource rents – if resources are extracted, the financial benefits flow to the whole population.

There are several major risks that stewardship might pose to indigenous peoples if it were applied to their land:

□ *Privatisation of common property*. Colonial governments have been highly reluctant to recognise common rights to territory and, where they have recognised the property rights of indigenous peoples it has usually been as private property.

□ *Money economy*. Once stewardship is introduced, just as when taxation is introduced, people are drawn into the money economy to pay the fees or taxes. This is exacerbated by the payment of a Universal Income.

□ *Dispossession from the land*. If there is a requirement to pay stewardship fees, whether this is an obligation on individuals or on the whole population, there is always a risk that they may not be able to pay it and that the process of dispossession from the land will begin.

□ *Overdevelopment*. If the lands of indigenous peoples are currently protected from development by outsiders, there is a risk that the introduction of stewardship might lead to overdevelopment unless the planning regulations were sufficiently restrictive.

It would always be wise to give indigenous peoples the choice of opting out of the whole apparatus of stewardship, and indeed to assume that this is the agreement unless they choose to opt in. If, having done this, they need financial support this should be provided as a gift or grant from charitable or government sources, not as a Universal Income.

Natural resources

As long as we allow individuals and corporations to profit from securing resource rents, there will be violence (civil wars, turf wars) and corruption (the allocation of resource rents by bribery). Stewardship captures resource rents for the benefit of the whole population, thereby preventing the violence and corruption that result from the struggle to appropriate them for private purposes.

The destabilising effect of unequal distribution of natural resources, for example oil within Iraq, would be significantly reduced if there was a commitment to share an Environmental Dividend, funded from the resource rent of oil, across the whole country. This would ensure that everyone benefited equally from any reserves, wherever they are located. This sort of mechanism has been proposed in Africa (Nicholas Shaxson 2007) and been put in place within the state of Alaska.

It would not be easy, or perhaps even possible, to reach such an agreement in most of oil-producing nations. But if we could agree about how we would ideally like to handle the wealth of the natural world, such as the resource rent for oil, it is always possible that an opportunity for implementing this may present itself.

Using the revenue

Just as in a high-consumption economy, in low consumption economies stewardship fees fund government spending and provide a Universal Income. Revenue from permits for the use of renewable resources is distributed as an Environmental Dividend and revenue from the use of non-renewable resources is invested in development of alternatives.

In a low-consumption economy, how much should be distributed as a Universal Income and how much should be spent by the government on locally appropriate development to provide public goods? And what sort of public goods? Decisions about spending are probably best carried out at community level not nationally or internationally. Corruption and the dominance by special interests can be minimised by imposing simple conditions, such as the requirement that people hold local meetings to decide spending priorities and that they publicly present the accounts for the spending. The condition that needs to be imposed at national level is that governments seeking election declare (and respect) the level of Universal Income that they will pay during their term of office. This requires them to decide in advance the maximum proportion of the total stewardship fees that they will use for collective purposes.

It is not possible to prescribe the right balance between Universal Income and spending on public goods, but it seems likely that while transfers are relatively small and infrastructure poorly developed, the most productive use of the revenue might be to provide appropriate public goods.

On the other hand, a Universal Income would be a powerful way to reduce absolute, and even relative, poverty. One example would be the care for orphans in sub-Saharan Africa. Here the young adult population was decimated by AIDS and many families found themselves bringing up not only their own children but several sets of nephews and nieces with no additional resources. A Universal Income paid to each child as well as to each adult would ease the financial burden and support a non-institutional mechanism for providing care for orphans. The experience of distributing a Universal Income in Namibia provides grounds for optimism that this approach would bring significant benefits in terms of increased use of education and health care, improved nutrition and business development.

In summary: Stewardship brings to low-consumption economies the same sorts of social and economic benefits as it does to high-consumption economies, including revenue for government spending and the security of a Universal Income. This may be supplemented by International Stewardship.

Capturing resource rents from oil and other natural resources for the benefit of everyone offers revenue for the government to invest in the future or distribute as Environmental Dividend and removes an important underlying cause of conflict, corruption and the export of wealth by the rich. Each of these impacts contributes to the reduction of poverty and inequalities.

Part III Distribution of wealth

Chapter 8 Inequalities

There are many ways in which people are unequal. These include their education, housing, employment, power, wealth and income and wealth. This chapter focuses on inequalities in income, largely because a wide range of social problems have been shown to be worse in countries where income is unequally distributed. These include:

❑   homicide, violent crime and domestic violence

❑   discrimination by race, ethnicity, gender and class

❑   poor social cohesion and involvement in community life

❑   low levels of trust

❑   poor educational attainment

❑   lower life expectancy

❑   health problems including obesity, drug and alcohol dependence and teenage pregnancy. (Wilkinson 2005)

The chapter describes an ownership economy from the perspective of social rank, the distribution of income, the causes and impact of inequalities and intergenerational inequalities. It then sets out how a stewardship economy could change all of this by providing everyone with equal access to land and natural resources, and by distributing the wealth provided by the natural world to everyone, equally, as a small private income.

Ownership economy

Social rank

Richard Wilkinson (2005:22) suggests that there are two fundamentally different ways in which people manage the competition for scarce resources, each of which is also found in other primates. One is a dominance hierarchy, in which the most powerful individuals establish the highest rank and are accorded priority – for food, space, a mate or whatever – while the weakest receive what is left over. The other is a co-operative relationship in which members of a group recognise each other's needs and engage in gift giving, food sharing, and reciprocity. Our species employs a mix of the two, but the dominance hierarchy is never far from the surface.

A dominance hierarchy is based on many sources of power – and, thus, dimensions of rank – in human societies. These include gender, ethnicity and education. Each of these will count for more, or less, in any particular situation. Income and wealth are important components of rank and provide priority access to scare resources. Even a simple economy creates income inequalities and, thus, social ranking.

Income distribution

Wealth is distributed in a fat-tail distribution – one in which small numbers of very rich people own a very high proportion of the wealth. For example, one percent of the U.S. households at the top of the wealth distribution possess around one third of the total U.S. household wealth (Arthur Kennickell, 2007). This same distribution is found across a wide range of societies and historical times.

Why are human societies so unequal?

Is it because one group or class exploits another, as those on the left generally believe? Or is it caused by the differences in people's attributes, skills and diligence as held by those on the right?

Exploitation and individual differences no doubt play a part. But it is astonishing to see the way in which inequalities in income and wealth arise very reproducibly in computer simulations of remarkably simple economic models in which there is no exploitation and only tiny differences between individuals. Eric Beinhocker (2007:80) describes the agent-based model called Sugarscape, constructed by Joshua Epstein and Robert Axtell, in which artificial agents require sugar as a source of energy and they die if they fail to acquire enough sugar. They differ amongst themselves in their metabolism and vision. In the most basic version, agents are able to look for sugar, move around and eat sugar. From a starting situation in which both wealth (sugar) and genetic endowment (vision) are randomly distributed amongst the agents, one might expect that there would be a random distribution of wealth at the end of the run of the model. In fact, 20 per cent of agents end up owning 80 per cent of the sugar. In real life, large numbers of people end up poor with a smaller middle class and much smaller group of super-rich. The Sugarscape model reproduces the fat-tail distribution.

There is no simple explanation – the dynamics of the simulation simply cause the lives of different agents to diverge widely. Small initial differences, and luck, lead to massive differences in outcomes. Allowing the agents to trade does nothing to reduce inequalities – indeed, while trading increases the average levels of wealth, it also increases the degree of inequality. Sugarscape teaches us that inequalities are not simply due to the factors that are usually blamed by left-wingers or right-wingers – exploitation of the poor by the rich or individual inadequacy.

Even though inequalities in income, wealth and rank may be natural phenomena, this does not mean that they are unavoidable or desirable. Danny Dorling, in his magnificent book *Injustice: why social inequality persists* (2010: 5) argues that inequalities persist because of five underlying beliefs: that elitism is efficient; exclusion is necessary; prejudice is natural; greed is good, and despair is inevitable. If we choose to do so, we can reject these beliefs and build a society with greater equality of income and wealth.

The impact of inequalities

There is a growing body of evidence that unequal societies are more dysfunctional than more equal ones according to most measures of health, violence, discrimination, social capital and happiness (Richard Wilkinson 2005). Although this represents the current consensus the underlying statistical methods, particularly the way in which outliers are treated in regression analysis, have been challenged (Peter Saunders 2010: 29).

Health

The World Health Organization (Commission on the social determinants of health 2008:2) concluded that inequity in the way that society is organised results in an unequal distribution of health and well-being.

It identified three arenas for action: improving the conditions of daily life; measuring and understanding the problem and assessing the impact of action; and tackling the inequitable distribution of power, money and resources.

Within any country, the more you earn the more likely you are to be in good health and to live longer. If you look at the map of any city the areas with highest life expectancy are the areas with the highest levels of income, which are also the areas of highest land value. The life expectancy of a poor person is less than that of a rich person in the same country – by 15–20 years in the U.S., 5–7 years in the UK and less in Nordic countries (Richard Wilkinson 2005:14).

You might expect, then, that people living in a richer country would be, on average, healthier than people living in a poorer country. And that is exactly what you do find when you make a comparison amongst low-consumption and medium-consumption economies – those in which the average per capita Gross National Income was less than US$ 11,456 per year in 2007. The poorest countries do have the poorest health. Absolute poverty denies people access to necessary physical resources – food, clean water, sanitation, shelter and a safe environment. The major causes of death in these countries are under-nutrition, infectious diseases and injuries.

In high-consumption economies, people live longer and experience an entirely different pattern of illness; the major causes of death are cardiovascular disease, cancers, chest disease and injuries. The wealthy here, too, are healthier than the poor people in the same country. Differences in 'lifestyle factors' such as diet, smoking and exercise explain part, but only part, of the difference between rich and poor in these economies.

The surprise comes when you make a comparison amongst high-consumption economies. The richer high-consumption countries are, on average, no healthier than the poorer high-consumption economies (Richard Wilkinson 2005:68). This puzzle – that in any country the wealthy are healthier than the poor, but wealthy high-consumption economies are no healthier than poorer high-consumption economies – can be explained by the direct impact of income inequalities within those countries (Richard Wilkinson 2005:106). The poor health of poorer people in high-consumption economies is not due *absolute* poverty and the lack of physical resources but, rather, to *relative* poverty (Peter Townsend 1979) and low social rank.

Income inequality within a society damages health, whether you compare countries around the world or states within the U.S. Inequality is associated with premature mortality and a wide range of specific health problems, including obesity, cardiovascular disease, alcohol and drug dependency, and teenage pregnancy. Inequalities worsen almost all the health problems that have been studied – apart from suicide, which is more common in more equal societies.

People of high rank are more in control of their own lives and work than are people of low rank. They are more likely to feel socially secure, valued and appreciated. We experience ourselves through our relationships with others, and how they see us is central to our well-being. Measures of health provide insights into how our society provides, or fails to provide, the social conditions for a satisfying life. Inequalities damage the quality of social relationships.

Murder and other forms of violence

Low-ranking people are more likely to be treated with disrespect than high-ranking people. They are more likely to have their personal worth, pride and dignity challenged, so it is not surprising that hostility levels are higher in those U.S. cities that have higher levels of income inequality (Richard Wilkinson 2005:51).

Homicide was one of the first social indicators found to be related to income inequalities, both in international studies and within the U.S. The impact of inequalities is enormous – it accounts for the fivefold variation in homicide rates between states in the U.S. (Richard Wilkinson 2005:48).

Discrimination

People from areas with high levels of income inequality score highly on measures of racial prejudice. There is discrimination against women too, as measured both by political participation and earnings disadvantage compared with men (Richard Wilkinson 2005:51).

Social capital

'Social capital' is a composite measure of the levels of trust between individuals, social cohesion, involvement in community activities and willingness to play one's part in social life (Robert Putnam). When researchers compare different countries, or different states in the U.S, they find that people living in more egalitarian societies are more trusting than those in which there are large inequalities in income. They are also more likely to be involved in community life – in voluntary groups, shared activities, voting and reading local newspapers (Richard Wilkinson 2005:45). More equal societies have higher levels of social capital.

Happiness

Economists generally treat a person's happiness as if it were equal to the total cost of the products and services that they consume. But this is completely out of line with most people's experience, in which happiness is related to the relationships we have with our partner, family, friends and work colleagues and to our health and sense of security. Our financial situation and level of consumption is low down on the list.

Richard Layard (2005:41) quotes a study by Solnick and Hemmenway (1998: table 2) in which Harvard students were asked to choose between living in two imaginary worlds – one in which they earned US$50,000 a year and the average income was US$25,000, the other in which they earned US$100,000 a year and the average income was US$250,000. The majority preferred the first.

What hurts about poverty, once the necessities of food and shelter are provided, is being low down in the pecking order and not being able to afford what others can take for granted. Polly Toynbee (2008: 3) provides the metaphor of a camel train to describe income inequalities, with the rich out front. The Harvard students were choosing to put themselves near the front of the camel train. The comparisons that you make are those that you are able to make. It is possible to make comparisons with the stars of TV or magazines, but most comparisons are with your neighbours on the camel train. For a poor person, what hurts is not being able to afford a child's birthday present. For a rich person, it is not being able to afford private schooling or exotic holidays.

National and international studies of happiness show a remarkable similarity with those of health. Making comparisons amongst low-consumption economies, people in the poorest low-consumption economies are less happy than those in richer low-consumption economies. But, making comparisons amongst high-consumption economies, the average level of income makes no difference to happiness.

It is relative poverty that damages happiness in high-consumption economies. Even if inequalities were necessary for the creation of wealth, as some suggest, they don't increase people's happiness.

Perhaps we should all be asking ourselves something like a version of John Rawls' (1971) question: If we had no way of knowing our own attributes, preferences, qualifications or level of income and we were offered the choice between two worlds, which would we choose– a world in which income inequalities are large or one in which they are small?

Effect of income equality on quality of life

The surprising, and hopeful, finding about inequalities is that health and well-being are not zero-sum games in which one person's gain is another person's loss. Some of the reason for this is simply that £1000 makes more difference to the quality of life of a poor person than a rich person; so, transferring wealth from rich to poor improves the overall quality of life of the population. But it is more than this. Societies in which women's status is closer to that of men are characterised not only by better health for women, but also for men, too. Fewer poor people are the victims of violence in a more equal society, but fewer rich people are affected, too. All, except perhaps the 30 per cent who are most well off, are likely to live longer in a more equal society (Richard Wilkinson 1994).

Does social cohesion cause equality, or does equality bring about social cohesion? Are both cohesion and equality caused by some other factor, something about the way that we relate to each other that causes both?

Does income inequality cause ill health or does ill health cause inequalities? Richard Wilkinson (2005:205-212) provides examples that demonstrate that, over the course of time, changes in inequalities occur before the impact on health shows up. These include the deterioration in health in Eastern Europe as income inequalities increased and market reforms were introduced and the increase in social cohesion in the 'Asian Tiger' economies as they narrowed their income differences between 1960 and 1980. During World War II British government attempted to foster national unity and make it feel as though everyone was sharing the burden of war. Essentials were rationed, Income Tax was made more progressive and income differentials were dramatically reduced.

There is, however, a good candidate for the link between health and inequalities – rank itself, and the respect that it commands. If there is a way to increase the respect that people genuinely feel for each other, perhaps by promoting other forms of rank in our societies, this might reduce the dependence of health on equality of income. Even so, it is reasonable to expect that in a society with more equal incomes, people would have longer, healthier and happier lives, and would achieve more educationally. There would be lower levels of violence and homicide, discrimination and teenage pregnancy.

Significant improvements can be achieved well before reaching a state of anything like perfect equality. Death rates amongst men under the age of 65 are twice as high in the most unequal U.S. states as in the most equal ones, although the difference in inequality is not great – the proportion of total income received by the poorest half of the population is 18 per cent in the most unequal states compared with 24 per cent in the most equal states (Richard Wilkinson 2005:131).

There is growing discontent with the high levels of income inequality in ownership economies, particularly as the credit crunch of 2007 and the recession of 2008 was caused by the highest-paid financiers. Polly Toynbee and David Walker (2008) caught this mood in their appropriately named book, *Unjust rewards*.

Should we redistribute wealth?

Most people recognise some situations in which it seems right for the state to redistribute wealth from those who have enough to those who don't, even if only in emergency situations. But there are limits to popular support for this redistribution, particularly when financed from Income Tax, because it seems unfair to take wealth from those who have worked hard or taken risks and redistribute to those who have not.

120

If we are to tackle the many forms of inequality that run through our society we will need to do more than just redistribute wealth. We will have to arrive at a society in which the elite recognise that the 'others' are just as worthy of respect, power and wealth as they are themselves. Such a society would recognise, amongst many other things, that everyone has an equal right to the wealth of the natural world.

Intergenerational inequalities

The current situation in the UK is reminiscent of a game of Monopoly that has been running for hours when a new player joins the game. Most of the sites are owned, and the new player has a major challenge to escape paying rent for long enough to purchase somewhere of their own. Property is owned by the older generation and unaffordable to the young, even ignoring the additional burden of debt from their student loans.

Many young people have no option but to live in overcrowded rented accommodation, couch-surf or return to live with their parents in the hope of saving enough for a deposit on a house. This can be damaging to their development and to family relationships.

In summary: Inequalities in wealth and income occur in most economies and do not require as an explanation either individual inadequacy or exploitation. Inequalities are destructive to society and need active measures to reduce them. Ownership economies have only very unsatisfactory means to reduce inequalities (such as Income Tax with all its problems) and are becoming more unequal. We need a different and fair economy in which inequalities in income and wealth are substantially reduced.

Stewardship economy

Direct impact of stewardship on inequalities

The idea that inequalities in wealth and income are caused by unequal land ownership is not a new one (Jean-Jacques Rousseau 1755), and it is not surprising that a new approach to property rights in the natural world should offer the possibility of reduced inequalities.

While stewardship is intended to ensure that everyone benefits equally from the wealth of the natural world, it is not specifically designed to promote equality of income or wealth, but it seems highly likely that a stewardship economy would be far more equal than an ownership economy.

Stewardship redistributes the income stream that arises from the natural world, rent. As this rent is at present more concentrated in the hands of a small minority than total income, it would redistribute income more effectively than then the tax-benefit systems with which we are familiar in ownership economies. In addition, stewardship reduces tax avoidance and evasion, mainly the preserve of the rich, and removes the discrimination by the tax system in favour of those who own their homes. Universal Income enables those currently excluded from work to work as much or as little as they want, makes it easier for them to take on part-time work and reduces pay differentials.

The direct effect of a stewardship economy is to transfer wealth from those who use more than their equal share of the natural world, both land and the natural environment, to those who use less than their equal share. It transfers wealth from rich parts of the country to poor parts, from those with large homes in desirable locations to those with small homes in less desirable locations, from those who use a lot of natural resources to those who use less, and from businesses that use land and natural resources to all of us equally. So, the direct effect of stewardship is likely to be a society in which people's total income, including Universal Income and Environmental Dividend, is much more equal.

There is no guarantee though. Rich people might choose to live in small homes in less desirable areas to minimise their stewardship fees and to use less than their equal share of the environment to increase their net income from the Environmental Dividend. But it's not likely that many will follow this path – securing a desirable home, consuming natural resources and accessing the environment are all high on most people's spending priorities, particularly the rich.

Part-time work

A stewardship economy provides everyone with a small private income that makes it possible for people to choose part-time work rather than the current choice of either full-time work or benefits that are conditional on not working at all.

Pay differentials

Replacing conditional benefits with a Universal Income removes the unemployment and poverty traps and supports people as they take on work.

One of the elements that is not predictable about a stewardship economy is how much people would choose to work and to earn. Rates of pay for different jobs would change in ways that are uncertain, but it seems likely that wage differentials would narrow.

Intergenerational inequalities

Owning land carries the duty to pay stewardship fees, which means that tenants are not financially disadvantaged in relation to owner-occupiers. People can choose whether to live with the stability of a home that they own or the flexibility of a home that they rent. As owner-occupiers hoard less land, more is available on the market and its price, whether market value or market rent, is lower than in an ownership economy.

Access to the wealth of the natural world

At present those who make use of more than their fair share of the natural world pay very little for this, and the costs are externalised to the detriment of the planet and other people. In a stewardship economy those benefiting from a larger share of the natural world would pay environmental fees and charges and this revenue would provide some financial compensation to those who make use of less than their fair share – often, younger people.

Discount rates

Even if the older members of the electorate block the election of governments that will explicitly lower discount rates, interest rates are likely to be lower in a stewardship economy and so the future will be taken into account in decision-making.

Transition

Transition to a stewardship economy, particularly the removal of a progressive Income Tax, would need to be handled carefully to ensure that there were no temporary increases in inequality.

There will still be political differences about whether there should be additional measures to reduce inequalities. Liberal and socialist versions of stewardship might use Inheritance Tax to reduce the transmission of privilege from generation to generation. They might introduce a wealth tax and might retain a progressive Income Tax for as long as pay differentials remain as extreme as they currently are. But it is highly likely that, towards the end of the transition to stewardship, our economy would anyway be unrecognisably more equal.

A different basis for social ranking?

Even if income inequalities were the same in a stewardship economy as they are in an ownership economy, would they have the same sort of impact on social ranking as in an ownership economy? Rank depends on context: the highest ranking members of a closed religious order might be the most learned, the most pious, the most experienced, the most easy to get on with … but not the most wealthy. It is possible to imagine that in a stewardship economy in which more people chose to spend their time with their families, friends and communities rather than at work, high social rank might come to be associated with people's connection with their community rather than their wealth.

In summary: Stewardship could reduce inequalities to acceptable levels – not to equality perhaps, but at least to the level of a country such as Norway, where no child was growing up in poverty in 2003 (Stein Ringen 2007 quoted in Polly Toynbee 2008) .

Society in a stewardship economy would be more equal than in an ownership economy, and therefore likely to be healthier, happier, more trusting, cohesive, safe and secure.

Stewardship has an impact at a symbolic as well as at a practical level by claiming that we all have a right to a fair share of the natural world. It could have an impact, at this symbolic level, which goes far beyond the mere redistribution of wealth. It might even change the basis of social ranking so that this is based less on income and wealth and thereby undermine the elitism that underlies all inequalities.

Part IV Using the revenue from stewardship fees

Chapter 9 Universal Income

While this chapter considers the benefits of a Universal Income which apply in a stewardship economy, many of these apply also to an ownership economy. The next chapter looks at how a Universal Income could be implemented in a stewardship economy. There are other excellent books and reports with detailed and up to date information about Universal Basic Income.

Book 2 provides an overview of how to introduce a Universal Income, and the choices that could be made about the balance between Universal Income and replacement of taxes.

A Universal Income is a guaranteed (unconditional and automatic) income paid to every man, woman and child. It is not means-tested or contributory. Payment of Universal Income is not related to poverty, income or wealth, to an individual's work history or National Insurance contributions or to present work status or availability for work. It is not affected by marital status, gender, ethnicity or creed or the family unit or household in which the individual is living .

Universal Income is an independent income that provides a financial platform on which people can build lives of their own choosing, for example, part-time work, voluntary work, training or education.

The Universal Income described here is almost identical to what is known as Citizens' Income or Universal Basic Income. Citizens' Income or Universal Basic Income normally involve funding from general taxation and replace existing benefits.

Justification

We can consider Universal Income in terms of three broad justifications for any benefit: the right to survive, 'real-freedom-for-all' and the right to a share in the wealth of the natural world.

The right to survive

Most people accept that society has a collective responsibility for the survival of its members by ensuring that they are provided with at least the necessities for survival – water, food, shelter, clothing and primary health care. The Universal Declaration of Human Rights (United Nations) includes the right to 'A standard of living adequate for health and well-being'. But this approach can only ever justify a meagre level of Universal Income, and if this was the sole reason for providing a Universal Income there would be long-running arguments about whether it was too little to ensure survival or too high to be fair to those who are earning and funding it through taxation.

John Locke (1632 – 1704) recognised a general right to subsistence:

'Men, being once born, have a right to their Preservation, and consequently to Meat and Drink, and such other things, as Nature affords for their Subsistence' (Locke 1690 (a)) .

This view imposes duties on people to satisfy others' needs (or at least to stand aside while the needy make use of property acquired by those who are not needy):

'But we know God hath not left one Man so to the Mercy of another, that he may starve him if he please: God the Lord and Father of all, has given no one of his Children such a Property, in his peculiar Portion of the things of this World, but that he has given his needy Brother a Right to the Surplusage of his Goods; so that it cannot be justly denied him, when his pressing Wants call for it… And therefore, no Man could ever have a just Power over the Life of another, by Right of property in Land or Possessions…...As *Justice* gives every Man a Title to the product of his honest Industry….so *Charity* gives every Man a Title to so much out of another's Plenty, as will keep him from extream want, where he has no means to subsist otherwise'(John Locke 1690 (b)).

Real freedom for all

Philippe Van Parijs (1995 (a)) argues for a society that provides what he calls 'real-freedom-for-all', where each person has three things: security enshrined in a well-enforced structure of rights; self-ownership; and the greatest possible opportunity to do whatever they might want to do. He shows that, ignoring differences in individual abilities, this requires the highest unconditional income for all consistent with security and self-ownership (1995 (b)).

He considers the case of two people – Lazy, who spends his days surfing, and Crazy, who spends her days working. Van Parijs concludes that what would justify the taxation of Crazy, and transfer of benefits to Lazy, is if Crazy makes use of more than her fair equal share of natural resources. If she does so, it is justifiable to tax these resources to provide the revenue for an unconditional Citizen's Income for Lazy(1995 (c)).

His concern, however, is to equalise the assets each is endowed with so as to enable them to pursue their conception of the good life (1995 (d)), and he believes that this is the case whether these are naturally occurring assets or artefacts. He therefore advocates a range of additional taxes to fund a Citizen's Income – taxes on gifts, bequests, intellectual property and scarce jobs.

The right to a share of the natural world

Agrarian radicals and left libertarians have insisted that everyone has a right not just to subsistence but to an equal share of the natural world.

In a stewardship economy the level of the Universal Income is not determined by a judgement about what people need to survive or are prepared to pay, or about the highest level of transfer that does not harm security or self-ownership. The collection of stewardship fees is a fairer and more efficient way of allocating property rights in the natural world than ownership and Universal Income distributes the revenue.

Fairness to taxpayers

Reciprocity

A Universal Income funded from general taxation in an ownership economy is understandably seen as violating strong reciprocity (explained previously as conditional co-operation and punishment of those who violate the norms of co-operation). Why should anyone pay taxes to support even a small number of people who choose not to earn their share?

As stewardship fees are the compensation that is paid by a steward for excluding others from part of the natural world, distribution of the revenue from these fees as a Universal Income meets the criterion of strong reciprocity. In addition, the choice not to work or to work less (and so to consume less, contribute less to greenhouse gas emissions and so on) may come to be widely seen to be a desirable life choice.

Not corrupting the taxpayers

In a stewardship economy, the Universal Income is a right. It provides us all with compensation for our collective agreement to respect the rights of stewards to their land. Taxpayers are liberated from the sense of being robbed and from the invitation to make value judgements about other people's lives.

Fairness to recipients

How well does Universal Credit measure up against the criteria we used for assessing fairness to recipients in the current benefits system in the UK – respect, equal treatment of men, women and children, support for a variety of family structures and valuing unpaid work?

Respect

Universal Income is unconditional, so it avoids means tests and other intrusions associated with conditional benefit systems. People are unlikely to feel demeaned by receiving Universal Income. In part this is because there are none of the hurdles that deter potential beneficiaries in conditional systems. But most significantly, Universal Income is an automatic right not a conditional charitable hand-out. It does not come from the income of others who have worked for it but is a rightful share of our common wealth.

If additional benefits are paid to people with additional needs, the individual assessment might still be perceived to be demeaning. This is likely to be less problematic when entitlement to health-related and disability-related benefits are assessed as part of an overall assessment of a person's health and social care needs than when it is a stand-alone hurdle to gaining a particular benefit.

The assessment of eligibility of migrants could unfortunately be as odious and offensive in a stewardship economy as it is at present, though the amount of economic migration may reduce if more countries were to adopt stewardship and make reciprocal agreements.

Universal Income increases self-reliance by giving individuals what is rightly theirs, and this enables them to take responsibility for themselves in a way that would otherwise be impossible. It provides a financial platform on which they can build their work and lives.

Equal treatment of men, women and children

A Universal Income treats women and men equally and a stewardship economy recognises that children have a claim on the resources of the world in their own right. In a stewardship economy society as a whole bears a financial responsibility for its children. In its purest form a Universal Income would be paid at the same rate to children and to adults, in recognition of their equal right to the wealth of the natural world. During transition it is likely that for pragmatic reasons the level of Universal Income for a child would need to be lower than for an adult.

Support for a variety of family structures

A Universal Income is paid to individuals unconditionally, not to households, and gives each person the freedom to make their own choices about how to organise their lives. It is non-intrusive, non-judgemental and able to accommodate any living arrangements people may choose. A child's Universal Income provides them with a 'dowry' – instead of being a financial liability to the custodial parent, a child comes with their own income stream attached.

Valuing unpaid work

In a stewardship economy each individual has the right to a share of the wealth of the natural world, and this right is unrelated to present or past engagement in paid work in the formal economy. The whole distinction between paid and unpaid work is less clear in a stewardship economy than in an ownership economy as there is no Income Tax or unemployment benefit and so no need to account for earnings or divide people into 'employed' and 'unemployed'.

Universal Income is unconditional, so people are completely free to participate in the gift economy by volunteering or by taking on whatever unpaid work they choose.

Responsibilities of recipients

Minimum requirements

A person receiving Universal Income in a stewardship economy has duties and responsibilities. At the very least they need to accept the process by which stewardship fees are assessed, collected and distributed as Universal Income. This will require accepting the systems needed to a support a stewardship economy, i.e., legislative, administrative, judiciary and policing. And, since the value of land is influenced by the quality of many aspects of society, the beneficiary of the Universal Income shares some responsibility for maintaining the civic order.

While everyone has a right to share the wealth of the Earth and its natural resources, in a stewardship economy stewards also have a responsibility to care for the earth.

Reciprocal duties

There are choices to be made about whether the right to a Universal Income should carry with it reciprocal duties.

The quality of life for an individual depends on their being connected to society. In ownership economies, one of the most significant forms of connection has been through the contribution of paid work. The long-term unemployed in ownership economies have lost this connection, and there is a fear that people might become similarly disconnected if they are simply recipients of a Universal Income. It might be that, for the benefit of the individual, some conditions should be imposed on the recipient of the Universal Income that would require them to engage in some relationship with others in society.

Effectiveness

How far is a Universal Income effective when considered in relation to employment and self-employment, the relief of poverty and supporting the gift economy?

Employment and self-employment

In a stewardship economy the Universal Income supports low-paid families in a simple, non-intrusive, fair, effective and efficient way. It is effective because generally it encourages work, volunteering and self-reliance.

No unemployment or poverty trap

If Universal Income is introduced in addition to existing benefits it does nothing to remove the existing poverty and unemployment traps. In a stewardship economy Universal Income would replace existing benefits and would, in due course, abolish these the unemployment and poverty traps.

In an established stewardship economy, a person's Universal Income is not withdrawn as their earnings rise. During transition to a stewardship economy, even if the Universal Income is subject to income tax, the withdrawal rate is no more than the tax rate, for example, nil, 20, 40 or 50 per cent depending on earnings, thus avoiding the unemployment trap.

Flexible workforce

A Universal Income allows and encourages people to work in flexible ways that meet their own need to find the correct balance between paid work and the rest of their lives. It provides the reliable base of a small private income to which other earnings can be added.

In an economy where everyone receives a Universal Income, workers are more flexible – more ready to take time off to retrain and more ready to accept redundancy when it's necessary. Workers in a stewardship economy simply don't need the raft of job protection measures that are required in an ownership economy.

Low burden on employers

Universal Income is good for business, and so for employment. In a stewardship economy, stewardship fees replace all other taxes, so employers have a flexible workforce who receive Universal Income and cost less to employ as there are no employers' National Insurance contributions. Employers are also free from Corporation Tax, VAT and Income Tax.

Universal Income would have an unpredictable impact on the amount of work that people choose to do. For some people, particularly those with unsatisfying or unpleasant jobs or strong interests outside work, a Universal Income might make them less willing to work and allow them both to reduce their hours and to negotiate higher rates of pay.

The absence of taxes in a stewardship economy, particularly Income Tax and National Insurance Contributions, would, by contrast, provide a greater incentive to work as people receive the whole of their earnings. The greatest improvement in the incentive to work applies to low earners and the unemployed, who are spared the high withdrawal rates of traditional benefit systems and their unemployment and poverty traps. One of the most significant consequences of stewardship is that it transforms the incentives and rewards in a way that favours working.

This is not to suggest that this change in incentives is enough in itself to ensure full employment, or that people should be left unsupported if they want to work and find it difficult to do so. Libertarians might think that it is a matter of personal responsibility for people to acquire the skills necessary for employment and to fund this themselves, for example from their Universal Income. Liberals might recognise that a background of deprivation makes it difficult for people to achieve their full potential and so might ensure that additional funded education and training is made available. Socialists might do so as well, out of an additional recognition of the value to society of a well-educated and employable population.

Local Universal Income trials in Low Consumption Economies have increased the income that recipients have earned from work, mainly by providing them with capital. How a Universal Income would impact people's propensity to work in a High Consumption Economy is uncertain but should be clearer when current trials have been evaluated (see more in section on Trials of a Universal Income).

Relief of poverty

Women

A Universal Income treats men and women equally. No one loses any entitlement to the Universal Income if they take time out of work for any reason, including caring for children or family members. A mother's Universal Income provides her with financial support during pregnancy.

Children

A child's Universal Income would provide funding for their living expenses and perhaps contribute to the cost of their education, savings or pension contributions.

Those of a neoconservative persuasion might favour paying less to children than to adults, on the grounds that they are (or should be) part of a family unit in which the parents have a responsibility to support the children financially. Socialists and liberals might judge the needs of children to be greater than those of adults, on the grounds that they are unable to earn a living. They might want a child's Universal Income to be payable before birth, to provide for their needs at birth.

Families

Universal Income is unrelated to need and paid to each individual, irrespective of living arrangements or contractual status such as marriage or civil partnership. This enables people who want to live in a shared household, and so to reduce their living expenses and environmental footprint, to do so. There is no need for intrusive investigations into people's living arrangements and no penalties for marriage or other forms of co-habitation.

Parents of young children experience a tension between the desire to care directly for their children and the need for an income to support the family. The time of greatest need for income coincides for many people with the time when their children are young. A Universal Income for children as well as parents allows parents to choose the most appropriate balance for them between childcare and the rest of their own lives, including paid work.

It's not possible to predict the age at which people would choose to retire in a stewardship economy. In the absence of distortions introduced by the tax-benefit system, it is likely that more people would take on part-time work at all ages, and the notion of retirement would become much more flexible.

Universal Income provides a platform on which a private pension provision can be built in a stewardship economy, playing the same role as the Basic State Pension in an ownership economy. If the Universal Income is paid at the same rate to people of all ages it will not be enough on its own to provide for all the needs of all older people who do not have savings. Additional funding will be needed if they need social care at home or in residential homes.

Universal Income does nothing to discourage savings for later life, but it is not possible to predict whether increased income during working life would enable people to save more or whether the expectation of a guaranteed Universal Income in later life would reduce the amount of savings people set aside for their retirement, and so the levels of investment in the economy.

A libertarian version of stewardship might expect people to take responsibility for meeting their needs by saving during their working life to provide for their old age. Liberal and socialist versions might provide an age-related Universal Income. Or they might provide an additional income for all older people, on top of the Universal Income, by making compulsory deductions from the Universal Income during adult life that are made available to the citizen to invest in the pension plan of their choice.

Transition from an ownership economy would need to be carefully designed to ensure that no one was worse off than under current pension arrangements. But after transition is complete, or well-advanced, there is much to be said for very gradually rebalancing the Universal Income so that it becomes age-independent.

Sickness

In a stewardship economy everyone receives the Universal Income whether they are well, sick, or only well enough to work part-time. This provides a basic level of income during sickness and makes part-time work possible during convalescence and recovery.

There are many additional ways in which a stewardship economy might support those who are sick. Libertarian versions of stewardship might expect people to decide whether they need to insure against loss of earnings due to sickness. Insurance companies would be free to decide whether to exclude people or to charge them higher premiums if a risk assessment warranted it.

Socialist and liberal versions of stewardship would want to be sure that everyone received an additional income during times of sickness. Socialists might make sickness benefit available to all sick adults, funded from the government budget and so, ultimately, from stewardship fees. It might, or might not, be related to past work history and might, or might not, be payable after retirement age. Liberals might provide a voluntary insurance-based scheme in which insurance providers are barred from excluding or charging higher premiums to people with pre-existing conditions.

Disability

In a stewardship economy people with disabilities receive their Universal Income, and services to support them are provided in the same way as they are in ownership economies.

Liberal and socialist versions of a stewardship economy would pay some sort of additional disability support benefit to people assessed to have additional needs, funded from the government's budget. This might take the form of a consolidation and rationalisation of existing disability-related benefits.

A libertarian version of stewardship would reflect the conviction of libertarians that the state is not a suitable agent for making judgements about special cases. It would pay no more than the standard Universal Income to disabled people and expect that additional support would be funded from charitable giving. This might seem unfair to many but would still be compatible with the fundamental principle of stewardship, which is simply that all people have a right to an equal share of the wealth of the natural world.

Carers

In a stewardship economy both the carer and the person being cared for receive the full Universal Income. Liberal and socialist versions might make an additional payment to carers in recognition of their contribution to society, as a component of a package of disability support benefits and funded from the government's budget.

Travellers

In a stewardship economy everyone is guaranteed a Universal Income and they also have a responsibility to pay the stewardship fee for the land on which they live. This means that travellers would be drawn more closely into the formal economy and would pay a market rent for the use of registered travellers' sites.

Supporting the gift economy

There are likely to be significant numbers of people in both ownership and stewardship economies who are not in work, but in a stewardship economy many more of them may have made an active choice to live within the income provided by the Universal Income. Part-time work and portfolio careers would be more likely than the extremes of unemployment and full-time work in ownership economies and give people space to take part in the gift economy.

A Universal Income provides unconditional support for everyone, including those who care for friends and family, volunteer for a wide variety of causes or engage in educational, self-developmental, creative and spiritual activities. People are supported to play a part in this gift economy and help to release its abundance.

While there is evidence that people who are unemployed are less happy than those in employment, this is not the case for people who are voluntarily 'out of the labour force' (Layard 2005). This will be the situation made possible in a stewardship economy.

Efficiency

We can review Universal Income against criteria of efficiency – take-up rates, cost of delivery and risk of fraud.

In a stewardship economy there are no barriers to receiving Universal Income, and new recipients are recruited at birth or when residence is granted. There is no reason to suppose that its take-up rate would be less than the 98 per cent achieved by Child Benefit, and perhaps higher as the incentive to claim is higher.

The only costs of assessment for Universal Income, either to the benefit authority or to the recipient, are those necessary to prevent fraud. It is reasonable to suggest that the Universal Income, like Child Benefit, would cost no more than 1-2 per cent of the total to administer. Indeed, it is likely to be less than 1 per cent as the costs per person would be similar to Child Benefit while the benefit delivered would be higher. And, of course, it would cost far less to administer than the plethora of benefits it replaces.

As with a conditional benefit, Universal Income requires mechanisms to ensure that there are no claims on behalf of fictitious recipients. This may paradoxically be easier to achieve with a universal benefit than for benefits that are available to only some people as each recipient has one, and only one, claim. While no system could be guaranteed to be entirely proof against fraud, biometrics are providing increasingly sophisticated ways of confirming the unique identity of individuals. A Universal Income would certainly be subject to less fraud than any other benefit system.

Certainty

Universal Income in a stewardship economy provides the clearest imaginable example of a benefit that fully meets the criterion of certainty. Since the benefit is not withdrawable or conditional on other circumstances (financial, domestic) it is guaranteed to be paid automatically, provided that there is no fraud or no deductions by the courts.

The amount of the Universal Income that is paid does depend on the level of economic well-being of the country as a whole, as reflected in the sum of all stewardship fees. This will vary over the course of time and so is uncertain on a year-by-year basis, though in a way that makes sense to everyone. The only other variable is government expenditure.

There is another aspect to the certainty of a Universal Income: each person receives their own income for their own use. There is no question about how it is shared amongst the family unit. One of the reasons why Child Benefit has broad support is that it is paid directly to the person caring for the child and is therefore available directly for spending on that child.

The greater transparency of the Universal Income compared with existing benefits allows people a greater understanding of the basis of the benefit system which could be expected to command greater public support than we see in ownership economies.

Saving and self-reliance

The Universal Income is not means-tested so people with savings still receive the Universal Income, and saving is encouraged. People with savings and independent incomes benefit – including pensioners and families with children. However, in the longer term, living in a society that provides for people's needs in old age might make us need to accumulate less wealth to provide for care.

Population growth

A question may be raised about the impact of Universal Income and a stewardship economy on the size of population. Any prediction is fraught with uncertainty. Mortality rates should be lower in stewardship economies than in an ownership economy due to the lower levels of inequality. A Universal Income benefits women as much as men, reduces inequalities and provides income security in old age.

In low-consumption economies without adequate pension and social security arrangements, introduction of a stewardship economy with Universal Income might be expected to lower birth rates. This may be the result of several factors including improved levels of women's education, greater financial equality for women and a reduced need for children to provide economic security in old age.

The same is likely to be true in high-consumption economies, but a Universal Income could have an additional and opposite effect. If some people at present avoid having children for financial reasons, removing the financial penalties of child rearing would result in more births. It is even possible to imagine parents might have more children than they would otherwise choose to have in response to the financial incentive of a child's Universal Income. It is difficult to know how significant this effect might be. In high-consumption economies family size seems to be determined less by financial considerations than by the balance parents seek between their lives as individuals and their lives as parents.

If the introduction of a Universal Income resulted in population growth with all its adverse consequences, it might be necessary to reduce the amount of Universal Income paid to children.

In summary

Providing a Universal Income recognises that most people want to live a useful and meaningful life and that they know best how to achieve this, how to organise their own lives. Universal Income gives them access to their fair share of the wealth of the land and trusts that they can organise themselves.

Universal Income is a more effective and efficient system of distribution than conditional benefit systems because it enables people to choose to work full-time, part-time, for low pay or as volunteers as they wish. Universal income minimises barriers to uptake, is cheap to administer, minimises risk of fraud and does not discourage savings.

Chapter 10 Implementing Universal Income in a Stewardship Economy

There are many possible ways in which a Universal Income might be introduced in a stewardship economy. It could be paid in addition to the whole range of existing benefits, but its full advantages would be felt only if it was paid as an alternative. Both liberal and socialist versions of Universal Income would continue to provide some additional needs-based benefits, such as allowances to people with sickness and disabilities. Libertarian versions might choose not to pay needs-related benefits in addition to the Universal Income.

In a stewardship economy the revenue from stewardship fees is used for government spending, then the remainder is distributed amongst the whole population - sharing out to everyone their rightful portion of the 'common treasury for all', the market rent of the land. The level of Universal Income is determined by the market rent of the land, not by the need of the recipient. Universal Income replaces many traditional benefits including Child Benefit, State Retirement Pension and Jobseekers Allowance.

This chapter describes Universal Income in an established steady-state stewardship economy. During transition from the benefits system in an ownership economy to a stewardship economy, care would be required to ensure that no one in receipt of benefits is worse off than they are now. Transition will likely consist of a combination of removing orthodox taxes and introducing a Universal Income that is accompanied by both a partial withdrawal of existing benefits and is subject to Income Tax while this remains.

Eligibility

The state collects the stewardship fees and decides who is, and who is not, eligible for Universal Income. Here are some of the options to consider and some possible choices:

Citizenship

One possibility is to make all citizens of a country eligible for its Universal Income – which is why a very similar proposal is often referred to as a Citizen's Income. People who have dual citizenship would need special treatment to ensure that they do not receive more than their fair share.

Residency

A residency qualification might be based on past residency, present residency or both. This could be in addition to a citizenship requirement, or as an alternative.

History of past residency

What level of Universal Income should be payable to someone who has lived for only some of their life in the country of current residence? The government of a stewardship economy will need to consider this and negotiate reciprocal arrangements with other countries that adopt stewardship.

One alternative is having no requirement for past residency – to pay the Universal Income in full to all those who have the current status of resident. But a country with no requirement of past residence for Universal Income would attract economic migrants. Another alternative is to introduce a threshold for qualifying. In the Alaska Dividend Distribution Programme people become fully eligible for the dividend once they have lived in the state for a year (Alaska Permanent Fund Corporation).

Alternatively, the Universal Income could be reduced in proportion to duration of residency but payable in each of the countries in which the person has been resident. A new resident to an index country would gradually accumulate the right to the Universal Income in that country – slowly for an adult, rapidly for a child. At the same time, they might retain a right to a diminishing level of Universal Income in their country of origin. This alternative would make the country less attractive to economic migrants.

If countries were to develop bilateral or multilateral agreements about eligibility for Universal Income, it should be possible for a person to 'pool' all their residence in the relevant countries and be eligible for a Universal Income in one of the countries.

Current residency

It would be possible to require that the person meet some requirement of current residency – for example, spending more than six months of the year in the country in question. Another option is to assess it on a daily basis, with the recipient eligible for 1/365 of a full annual Universal Income for each day they are resident.

An initial proposal for eligibility

A starting point for discussion might include conditions such as:

- Universal Income paid to anyone who is currently resident in the index country for more than six months each year, reduced in proportion to the amount of their life that they have been resident elsewhere

- residence in a country with which there is a reciprocal agreement is treated as if it 'counts' as much as residence in the index country

- people who have been granted asylum in an index country should be treated as though they have lived in that country for the whole of their lives (provided they are not receiving benefits from the country they have escaped from).

Reciprocal duties

A Universal Income could be paid entirely unconditionally, or it might be conditional on the recipient carrying out certain duties as an act of reciprocity. Libertarians might favour a version that has no qualifying requirements. A socialist might favour, say, 10 days of 'national service' (service to the state that might be military or non-military) per year. A liberal might favour the contribution of 10 days per year to others through a mechanism such as a Time Bank.

Paying Universal Income

How much Universal Income?

The level of Universal Income in a stewardship economy is set not by any judgement about what would be the 'right' level but, rather, by the revenue generated from stewardship fees minus the expenses of central and local government. The level of Universal Income is difficult to predict with any accuracy, partly because calculating total stewardship fees requires information about the current market rent of the land and partly because a stewardship economy is a complex system in which many of the choices that people would make are essentially unknowable. [1]

This section focuses on three scenarios for introducing Universal Income and explores who would be advantaged and disadvantaged by a Universal Income introduced in addition to or as an alternative to existing benefits. The illustrative figures given below assume that all the £180 billion revenue from stewardship fees is used for Universal Income.

The simplest case to consider is in an economy where there are no existing property rights. While transition from an established ownership economy to a stewardship economy needs to be gradual, to estimate the possible impact of a stewardship economy, Book 2 sets out thought experiments that describe an instantaneous switch from ownership to stewardship in the UK. These include the use of the revenue to:

- provide a Universal Income in addition to existing benefits

- provide a Universal Income as an alternative to existing benefits

- provide a Universal Income that is subject to Income Tax and partial withdrawal of benefits

---

[1] Editor's note: Widerquist (2020) suggests that the net cost of a Universal Income for the United Kingdom (not a stewardship economy) would be £67 billion per year (about 3.4% of GDP), enough to provide an annual income of £7,706 for adults and £3,853 for children. About 70% of families would benefit and for these families the average increase in income would be £4,056. The proportion of families with incomes below the recognised poverty line would fall from 16 percent to 4 per cent and all children and pensioners would rise above this line.

In a real transition the gradual introduction of stewardship fees equal to the increase in market rent (over at least 25 years) would reveal the amount of revenue available at every stage.

The estimates provided in this chapter would need to be replaced by detailed microsimulations to discover the impact of each option for a wide range of different households. It is almost certain that the ideal choice would be some combination of these, or indeed other, options.

Universal Income in addition to existing benefits

In the 'addition scenario' *all* existing benefits are retained, and the Universal Income is paid in addition to these. The Universal Income could be an equal payment for each person, or it could be age-related. The following chapter explores the justification for and wider benefits of a Universal Income in a stewardship economy.

Age-independent Universal Income

Stewardship suggests that the Universal Income should be distributed on an equal basis no matter what the recipient's age. If the available revenue were to be distributed in equal shares to all the 61 million inhabitants of the UK, each person would receive an additional income of about £3,000 per year (£2,950 per year or £56.74 per week).

Age-related Universal Income

It is, however, consistent with the principles of stewardship for the Universal Income to be age-related, particularly if this is necessary to ease transition. The £180 billion revenue could provide a Universal Income in addition to existing benefits at the levels shown below (Table Column 5). These levels are about two thirds of the amount the current benefit system considers to be adequate for survival – the maximum level of benefit available in an ownership economy (Child Benefit + Child Tax Credit, Income Support or Pension Credit, depending on age).

	UK population			Cost of UI		
	thousands	thousands	millions			
age	M	F	Total	UI pp pw	UI pp pa	Total cost (bn)
up to 1	404	385	1	£56	£2,922	£2
1 to 17	6,319	6,013	12	£49	£2,556	£32
18-24	2,998	2,851	6	£43	£2,239	£13
25-59	14,332	14,513	29	£43	£2,239	£65
60-64	1,778	1,861	4	£87	£4,527	£16
65+	4,321	5,609	10	£101	£5,237	£52
Total	30,151	31,232	61			£180

Calculating the cost of Universal Income for UK

Who benefits from Universal Income as an addition?

Introducing Universal Income as an addition to existing benefits and tax credits in a stewardship economy means that everyone benefits immediately that the first payments are made, including the poorest people currently receiving the highest levels of benefit.

In the simplest case of an age-independent Universal Income, every man, woman and child benefits from a private income of about £3,000 per year. The immediate impact of introducing stewardship fees at 100 per cent of market rent combined with a Universal Income will have different impacts on each household, but there are broad differences between tenants, landlords and owner-occupiers.

Tenants

Tenants are not liable to pay stewardship fees. There is general agreement that, unless the income of tenants increases or the landlord had set the rent at below market rates, landlords cannot pass their stewardship fees on to their tenants through increase in rent because an immediate rise in rent would force a tenant out and a landlord would forfeit their income. So, the short term impact on tenants is that each person benefits by about £3,000 per year. This is, however, only the immediate impact. See below.

Landlords

Most landlords also own their own home. They can be considered to be both landlord and owner-occupier, and their Universal Income taken into account in relation to their owner-occupation. Landlords pay stewardship fees, and assuming that about half the market rent of each property is the market rent of the land (the other half that of the buildings and other improvements), the immediate impact is that they lose about half their previous income. This, as with tenants, is the immediate impact.

Owner-occupiers

Consider a single person who own a modest home that has a market rent of about £6,000 per year (£3,000 per year for the market rent of the land assuming that half the value is in the land and half is in the building). They will receive as much in Universal Income as they pay out in stewardship fees. A couple will receive twice as much, and if they have two children they will receive £12,000 per year.

Universal Income as an alternative to existing benefits

It would be possible to imagine introducing the Universal Income and withdrawing existing benefits on a pound-for-pound basis. In this scenario people's total income from Universal Income and residual benefits would be unchanged. It would seem unfair that the poorest members of society, those on benefits, do not benefit from the introduction of the Universal Income. Those of them who do not own land would, on the other hand, be paying none of the stewardship fees. But benefit recipients who own land, and there are many recipients of the Basic State Pension in this category, would be hard hit by the need to pay stewardship fees while receiving no net benefit from Universal Income.

The big advantage of introducing Universal Income as an alternative is that people whose benefits were, in an ownership economy, conditional on unemployment or poverty now receive an unconditional income. They can work and earn with all the benefits this brings to them individually and to the economy as a whole.

The disadvantage is that this has some distributional effects that are not ideal. The position of a landlord is the same as when the Universal Income is introduced as an addition to existing benefits, although there may be a difference following that time. Tenants benefit 20 to 40 per cent less from the 'alternative' / reform scenario than they would from the 'addition' scenario, unless they are amongst the group who are not currently eligible for benefits but also earn too little to pay tax. In this case they benefit from the full Universal Income.

Owner-occupiers, like tenants, benefit less from this scenario unless they too are off benefits and their income too low to incur tax. Homeowners with above-average value homes will be disadvantaged by introducing Universal Income as an alternative to existing benefits, as will many single people throughout the country, even in a home whose value is below the local average and many couples throughout the country living in a home whose value is above the local average couples in the south living in a home whose value is above the local average.

Single owner-occupiers who are currently eligible to receive means-tested benefits will likely be disadvantaged.

Universal Income subject to Income Tax and partial withdrawal of benefits

This scenario is intended to illustrate a half-way house between introducing the Universal Income as an addition to existing benefits and introducing it as an alternative. Here the Universal Income is introduced with the intention that it will ultimately replace most benefits (other than for disability, carers, maternity and perhaps sickness. The underlying principle would be that no one suffered a reduction in their overall income as the result of this reform.

152

One way of achieving this would be for some percentage – say, 40 per cent - of each person's Universal Income to be deducted from the benefit package of their household. To take as an example, a family of two adults and two children on benefits receive a new total income of £12,000 per year from their Universal Income; £4,800 per year (40 per cent of £12,000) would be deducted from their existing package of benefits. This would still leave them £7,200 per year better off than they had been. The £4,800 per year that the government recovers, either in reduced benefits or in Income Tax, could be used to increase the total resource available for general distribution as Universal Income.

Impact on households

Here are some further examples of how individuals might be affected during transition to a stewardship economy:

A is a single person, in work and receiving no benefits. She earns £40,000 per year and bought her home recently for £120,000 (UK average in 2002), paying £6,000 per year in mortgage interest. The market rent of her land is rising by £500 per year (equivalent in an ownership economy to a rise in capital value of 5 per cent).

From the onset of transition, she faces a growing expenditure on the stewardship fees for her home of £500 per year, but she also benefits from a slowly growing Universal Income and from tax cuts that broadly compensate her. The big change is that her home is no longer an investment but a slowly depreciating asset.

B & C are a professional couple with a child of 4 years old. They bought their home recently for £480,000, paying £24,000 a year in mortgage interest. They receive child benefit but no other benefits. The market rent of their land is rising by £2000 per year (equivalent in an ownership economy to a rise in capital value of 5 per cent).

As land values rise they begin to pay a stewardship fee that rises by £2000 per year. They benefit from cuts in VAT and so on, and all three receive a Universal Income, though this is taxed as income. Their benefit package is reduced by 33p for every £ of Universal Income they receive. So, when the total family income from Universal Income is three times their original benefit package (1.8 times more once income tax has been paid at 40 per cent), they stop drawing child benefit. This occurs when the individual Universal Income is equal to the previous level of child benefit – if they had 2 children it would occur when the individual Universal Income is ¾ of the original level of child benefit.

D is a single person who earns £12,000 per year, gets no benefits and pays £5,000 per year in rent.

As the market rent of the land on which her home is located rises by £400 per year from the onset of transition, her rent rises accordingly. The difference from an ownership economy is that tax cuts and the Universal Income broadly compensate her for the increased rent.

If she was living in a more expensive home – or, rather, a home that increased in market rent by more than £400, she would do worse. If in a less expensive home, she would benefit even more.

The increased rent enables the landlord to pay the stewardship fee. But the landlord makes no additional profit as rents go up, and her asset is gradually depreciating

E & F are a couple with two children. They earn £18,000 a year from employment and receive child benefit and working families tax credit. They pay £7,000 per year in rent.

As the market rent of the land on which their home is located rises by £500 per year from the onset of transition, their rent rises accordingly. The difference from an ownership economy is that tax cuts and the Universal Incomes (4* £X) broadly compensate them for the increase in rent. Their benefit package of £Y (two child benefits and the working families tax credits) is reduced by 33p for every £ of Universal Income they receive.

So, when the total family income from Universal Income is three times their original benefit package (2.4 times more once income tax has been paid at 20 per cent), they stop drawing child benefit.

If they were living in a more expensive home – or, rather, a home that increased in market rent by more than £500, they would do worse. If in a less expensive home, they would benefit more.

The increased rent they pay enables the landlord to pay the stewardship fee. But the landlord makes no additional profit as rents go up, and her asset is gradually depreciating.

G is a single parent with children of 8 and 10. She rents her home. She receives child benefit, working families tax credit, housing benefit etc.

As the market rent of the land on which her home is located rises by £500 per year from the onset of transition, her rent rises accordingly. The difference from an ownership economy is that tax cuts and the Universal Incomes (4* £X) broadly compensate for the increase in rent. Her benefit package of £Y (two child benefits and the working families tax credits) is reduced by 33p for every £ of Universal Income she receives. So, when the total family income from Universal Income is three times their original benefit package (2.4 times more once income tax has been paid at 20 per cent), she stops drawing child benefit.

As in previous examples, if G was living in a more expensive home – or, rather, a home that increased in market rent by more than £500, she would do worse. If in a less expensive home, she would benefit more. The increased rent they pay enables the landlord to pay the stewardship fee. But the landlord makes no additional profit as rents go up, and her asset is gradually depreciating.

Mitigation during transition

In a long-established stewardship economy, one that had been in place for generations, people would be accustomed to saving for their old age and to moving to smaller homes as their income fell on retirement. The housing provided would allow this to happen easily, with many more mixed developments suitable for people at all stages of life.

During transition to stewardship, people would face difficult choices. Households on higher incomes would have to decide whether to pay the stewardship fee for their home or to move to a less expensive home. It will be important not to put people under undue pressure to leave their family home. If they decide to stay, it would be important to allow them to be able to draw down the capital tied up in the building that they own to pay their stewardship.

But during the transition to stewardship even the hybrid scenario has the disadvantage that it penalises certain people, including those who live alone, or are asset-rich and income-poor or receive means-tested benefits like pension credit. These impacts would be mitigated by the gradual transition to stewardship, an extension of Housing Benefit to owner-occupiers and the ability to choose between traditional benefits and the Universal Income.

The proposed transition to a stewardship economy (see Book 2) is very different from the thought experiment described above. Stewardship fees are set not at the market rent of the land but at the *increase* in the market rent of the land that has occurred since the onset of transition. This gives time for people to react to the coming changes.

Owner-occupiers are not currently eligible for Housing Benefit as they do not pay rent. During transition only, eligibility for Housing Benefit may need to be extended to owner-occupiers for the limited purpose of enabling them to pay their stewardship fees (not their whole housing costs) for an appropriate category of dwelling.

During transition, each household must have the option of choosing whether all its members receive the Universal Income or whether the household receives its existing benefits. It will be important to ensure that the value of these existing benefits is not eroded. They need to be indexed year on year (in line with earnings not prices). And benefits that are currently conditional on payment of National Insurance Contributions need to be retained even after these contributions have been phased out.

This would provide a clear guarantee that no one would be worse-off, and households would be free to choose how they are supported. Different households will find it beneficial to transfer to Universal Income at different stages, with those on the lowest levels of benefit transferring earlier than those on higher levels.

Next steps – a microsimulation exercise

This chapter has provided a limited illustration of how the revenue from stewardship fees could be used, and some sense of the challenges.

Any serious proposal to introduce stewardship fees would need to be very thoroughly explored by modelling its consequences for a wide variety of different sorts of households. The 'back of the envelope' calculations in this chapter suggest that a fair and effective proposal will be likely to consist of some combination of the removal of orthodox taxes and the introduction of a Universal

Income that is accompanied by both a partial withdrawal of existing benefits and is subject to Income Tax while this remains.

EUROMOD is a public domain microsimulation model of the UK (and other EU) tax-benefit systems. It was developed to explore the impact of changes in the tax-benefit system on households of different types. It will be necessary to use this, or similar, model, to identify the gains and losses of different sorts of household in order to fine-tune the design of transition.

Chapter 11   Investing in infrastructure

Infrastructure, for example transport infrastructure, improves business efficiency, labour productivity and Gross Domestic Product (GDP). Investment in public transport also reduces inequalities in income, and reduces the environmental damage caused by transport.

When a government funds transport infrastructure from general taxation this may feel unfair. Why should we all, as taxpayers, pay for local transport measures in parts of the country that we may never visit? It might seem fair if everyone benefited equally, but transport systems always have different impacts at different locations. Why can't the people who benefit meet the cost of the infrastructure?

This chapter suggests that infrastructure can become locally self-funding by laying claim to revenue from the increase in the market rent of the land that benefits from its provision. Ways of capturing the uplift in land value are compared in book 2 and the practical arrangements for managing infrastructure are described elsewhere.

Ownership economy

In ownership economies the costs of constructing and operating transport infrastructure fall on both users and the taxpayer. In addition, ways have been found to extract contributions from the other group who benefit from good transport connections – those who benefit from an increase in the value of their land.

Operating costs

The operating costs of transport systems include labour, maintenance, ticketing and the rental or capital costs of both fixed and mobile infrastructure. All or part of these costs may be met from charges to the direct users through ticket prices and tolls, though the transport operator is often able to provide the level of service that society wants only as the result of a state subsidy – that is to say, transport provision is prone to suffer from market failure.

Construction costs

Even when the revenue from fares is enough to meet the operating costs of transport provision, it is generally not enough to service the debt incurred in making an investment in transport infrastructure. The return on capital that investors anticipate is often not realised. Early investors in the canals, railways and the channel tunnel all saw the value of their shares fall dramatically (Fred Harrison 2006a). This has meant that governments have often had to step in to fund transport infrastructure because it provides a public good.

When the fullest possible assessment of the costs and benefits is carried out, the benefits may significantly outweigh the costs. The canals and railways were failures only for their investors. The landlords, who were the original sponsors of the schemes, were the real beneficiaries. Their mines and businesses flourished, and the market rent of their land soared, as their cost of transport to market fell. Many of them sold their transport shares on to a wider group of investors and it was these shareholders who lost out as the gains in land values were external to the finances of the canal and railway companies (Fred Harrison 2006a).

Infrastructure increases land values

The people who most obviously benefit from transport infrastructure are those who use it, and this is reflected in their willingness to pay to travel. But there are other beneficiaries including firms, workers, customers and landowners.

The value of a plot of land depends above all on its location and reflects the sum of all the services and opportunities that are available at that location. The improved job opportunities, trading opportunities, and quality of life provided by the transport infrastructure all increase the desirability of living and producing in this location.

When land becomes more desirable because of improved transport connections, its value rises. Building plots are worth more when they are served by roads. And when a rail link is built between a suburb and its city centre people living in the suburb can more easily work in the city centre, the suburb becomes a more desirable place to live, and the land values rise. The city centre becomes more accessible to workers, clients, customers and suppliers and land values rise there too. Landowners are the main financial beneficiaries in an ownership economy.

Not all landowners, however, gain from transport infrastructure. Negative impacts are also translated into land values – properties along a railway line may have higher levels of noise and pollution and this may reduce their value even if properties near stations rise in value. But for a well-conceived scheme the overall benefits outweigh the costs.

The idea of funding the development of transport infrastructure from the anticipated increase in land values has a long history. A witness to the Standing Committee on Metropolitan Communication suggested in 1845 that 40 year loans for transport infrastructure should be secured on the rise in rateable value of nearby property (Nicholas Crafts and Timothy Leunig 2006: 33).

In his illuminating book on self-funding transport infrastructure *Wheels of Fortune*, Fred Harrison describes the 1988 plans for the development of Canary Wharf in London's Docklands (Fred Harrison 2006a:64). The developers, Olympia and York, estimated that a new underground line to bring commuting workers from Waterloo and London Bridge main line stations would increase the market rent of the office space by £320 million per year, equivalent to an increase in its capital value of £3.2 billion. The estimates they obtained for the construction of the underground line were less than £600 million, and at this price they were willing to foot most of the bill for construction and hand the infrastructure over to the public sector to run. This solution foundered for several reasons including the increasing ambition of the scheme, disagreements about shares of funding, delays and ultimately an economic recession that dramatically reduced the demand for office space and so also reduced its projected market rent.

The proposed underground line was eventually completed in 1999 as the Jubilee line extension. Don Riley, a property developer with interests in the area, estimated in his book *Taken for a ride* (Don Riley 2001:23) that it raised property prices around the stations by £13 billion, more than three times its eventual construction cost.

Fred Harrison (1983) provides numerous examples of the increased land values resulting from infrastructure developments in ownership economies, including the Hokuso railway in Tokyo, the Metro in Washington and the Docklands Light Railway in London.

He also describes how speculative rises in land values can choke off development before it takes place. But measuring the change in land values associated with infrastructure developments is not easy and may in some cases demonstrate little or no change in land values. This was the case for the Sheffield and Croydon tram systems (RICS 2004), where local residents may not have viewed them as well-conceived infrastructure.

In ownership economies it is transport users and landowners who benefit from infrastructure investment, whether this is funded from private or public sources. If the transport provider relies for its income from transport users alone the venture may well not meet its costs and will either fail or require government subsidy. This suggests that we should capture the increase in land value that arises from the provision of well-conceived transport infrastructure, and use this revenue to subsidise transport investment and, if necessary, running costs.

When is it worth investing in transport infrastructure

Benefit: cost ratios

The narrowest assessment of benefits and costs is the purely commercial one of revenue and expenditure. Will the revenue from fares and tolls exceed the operational and maintenance costs plus the cost of repaying the capital investment? But many of the important benefits, and indeed costs, are experienced by others beyond the transport operating companies. Internalising these benefits and costs requires, first of all, a method for attributing a price to them.

The benefit of infrastructure investment to travellers can be quantified by establishing what they are prepared to pay for their journeys, either by observing their response to charges or by asking them in choice experiments. But it is a challenging task to put monetary values on all the other benefits and to aggregate these into some measure of the total benefit.

The benefit: cost ratio (BCR) provides an estimate of the net value of the benefit generated for every £1 invested (DfT 2012 accessed: 'New approach to appraisal'). In the UK this includes, in addition to revenue and expenditure, a monetary estimate of some additional social benefits such as the time saved, safety benefits and the costs of travel. It does not include GDP impacts or environmental costs or benefits.

The Department for Transport recommends that proposals for infrastructure investment should take, as the starting point for an assessment of their value for money, their benefit: cost ratio. The assessment is then adjusted to take into account non-monetised costs and benefits that include environmental and social impacts. Alternatively, a 'value for money benefit: cost ratio' incorporates monetary estimates of a wide range of social and environmental costs and benefits including GDP impacts, loss of amenity value of landscape and townscape, environmental damage to local air quality, greenhouse gas emissions, noise, accidents and congestion.

Value for money

In an ownership economy the deadweight loss of taxes on labour and enterprise depresses economic activity so any investment funded from general taxation must confer a substantial benefit to justify this loss.

In a private enterprise a real return on investment of 10 per cent, a ratio of benefits to costs of 1.1 to 1, would be worth considering. A government, mindful of its responsibility to manage the whole economy, can only invest if the benefits outweigh the costs to the economy as a whole, when the benefit: cost ratio is greater than 1.3 to 1 (assuming a deadweight loss of 30 per cent).

A project is judged to be:

- poor value for money if its BCR is less than 1 (loss-making)

- low value for money if its BCR is between 1 and 1.5 (a return on investment of up to 50 per cent)

- medium value for money if its BCR is between 1.5 and 2 (a return on investment of 50 - 100 per cent)

- high value for money if its BCR is over 2 (a return on investment of over 100 per cent (Department for Transport 2009).

Stewardship economy

In a stewardship economy appropriate investment in infrastructure leads to an increase in the value of land and so to an increase in stewardship fees. Most stewards of land that is affected by the infrastructure development will welcome its provision and accept the additional cost. Businesses will be able to pay this from the increased profits that the infrastructure brings, while householders will accept the cost for the additional utility that it provides. There will be some, however, who bear the costs but do not benefit.

Stewards who do not welcome improved infrastructure

A relatively small number of stewards will resist any proposed infrastructure investment because of the increased cost that this will impose. This is likely to be rare for businesses, as shown the voluntary supplementary business rate that contributed to the funding of Crossrail.

Householders are more likely to put up resistance. If they are themselves unlikely to make use of the infrastructure as they are being asked to pay higher stewardship fees for something they do not want. At its worst they may have to move home or see their area change as people who value the infrastructure, and can afford to pay for it, move in.

The position of householders close to the infrastructure is very different from what it would be in an ownership economy, where they would make a windfall gain as the value of their home increased. This is a real problem in for a stewardship economy but since a major purpose of a stewardship economy is to improve the efficiency with which land is used, the challenge can't be dodged. The most efficient use of land supplied with the new infrastructure is for it to be used by someone for whom the infrastructure is a significant asset. It is possible to put in place mitigating mechanisms during transition, such as rolling over payment of fees until the present occupant leaves the property. But as people adjusted to the multiple benefits of living in a stewardship economy their security would come less from owning a home that is rent-free and they would likely become more ready either to pay the increased fees or to move.

Self-funding transport

A business that is close to a transport link benefits from its ready access to markets, suppliers, other businesses and workers. The locational benefits enjoyed by its premises are reflected in the market rent of the land on which the business premises are located. When this revenue is pledged (hypothecated) to finance the infrastructure development, investment is funded by its beneficiaries – what Fred Harrison refers to as 'self-funding transport systems'.

In a stewardship economy everyone who benefits from transport infrastructure pays for the benefits they receive, whether this is as a traveller, a local business or a homeowner. Travellers pay fares and stewards whose locations benefit from the infrastructure, such as homes and businesses close to stations and transport intersections, pay higher stewardship fees.

Economists do not generally like hypothecated taxes because the revenue from the tax is likely to be either too little for the purpose identified, leading to underfunding, or too much, leading to wasteful spending. But hypothecation of stewardship fees to provide self-funding infrastructure provides the right amount of revenue – the amount that the infrastructure actually generates.

Government funding without deadweight losses

Where new infrastructure is planned, its benefits, of course, have to outweigh its costs in a stewardship economy, but the costs do not impose any deadweight loss as the revenue is raised from stewardship fees not taxes on income, profits and so on. The state in a stewardship economy would invest more in transport infrastructure because it could accept a 10 per cent return on investment rather than requiring a return of 50 per cent before a project is judged to be even of medium value for money.

An approach like this has been used in Copenhagen to finance its mass transit system (Tony Vickers 2007:30) from the Land Value Taxes anticipated from the development of the dockyards.

Utilities

In the same way that transport can be self-financing, if increases in land value are captured and used to fund transport provision, so the provision of other sorts of infrastructure like the utilities could tap in to the increase in land values that these produce.

Summary: In a stewardship economy transport infrastructure is funded not by taxes on the whole population but by charges paid by those who directly benefit from it, passengers and stewards of the land that is more desirable because of the transport provision. Infrastructure provision is effective because it is self-funding and is not held back by the imposition of deadweight losses on the economy. It is fair because stewards of the land, not taxpayers as a whole, benefit from the infrastructure and contribute to its cost.

www.ingramcontent.com/pod-product-compliance
Lightning Source LLC
Chambersburg PA
CBHW051213170526
45166CB00005B/1882

* 9 7 8 1 4 7 1 7 0 1 7 9 5 *